GET DIRTY

21 Lessons On Evangelism

GET DIRTY
21 Lessons On Evangelism

Josh Finklea
Foreword: Mark Moore

Pleasant Word
A Division of WINEPRESS PUBLISHING

© 2007 by Josh Finklea. All rights reserved.

Pleasant Word (a division of WinePress Publishing, PO Box 428, Enumclaw, WA 98022) functions only as book publisher. As such, the ultimate design, content, editorial accuracy, and views expressed or implied in this work are those of the author.

No part of this publication may be used or reproduced, stored in a retrieval system, or transmitted in any form by any means–electronic, mechanical, photocopying, recording, or any other—except for brief quotations in printed reviews, without the prior written permission of the publisher.

Unless otherwise noted, all Scripture quotations are taken from the *Holy Bible, New International Version*®. *NIV*®. Copyright © 1973, 1978, 1984 by International Bible Society. Used by permission of Zondervan. All rights reserved.

ISBN 13: 978-1-4141-0918-3
ISBN 10: 1-4141-918-0
Library of Congress Catalog Card Number: 2006910973

Contents

Foreword vii
Introduction xi

Chapter One: Dirty Jesus 17
   Don't be afraid of a little dirt.
Chapter Two: Be a S.T.A.R. 25
   Become a S.T.A.R. and you will see people come to Christ.
Chapter Three: Do You See Anything? 33
   Open your eyes and see people the way God does.
Chapter Four: Hell 39
   Hell is real. Will you save people from it?
Chapter Five: Gravity 45
   The weight will break you.
Chapter Six: Opportunity Knocks 55
   God ordains appointments for you. Will you be ready?

Chapter Seven: I Love Sinners 61
  Love transforms lives.
Chapter Eight: Selfish Christians 69
  When you see a person in need do you walk past or do you stop?
Chapter Nine: Eyes of Innocence 77
  Look deep into a person's eyes and see her soul.
Chapter Ten: Give Up 85
  If you want to follow Christ you have to be willing to give up everything.
Chapter Eleven: Don't Judge the Book 93
  Do you judge the book by the cover?
Chapter Twelve: I Love to Flirt 101
  Have you ever heard of spiritual flirting?
Chapter Thirteen: Rock Bottom 109
  When people hit rock bottom, give them God.
Chapter Fourteen: I Hate Religion 117
  Do you hate organized religion?
Chapter Fifteen: Empty 125
  We all have holes in our hearts that need to be filled.
Chapter Sixteen: This Is War 133
  We are at war. Are you ready to fight?
Chapter Seventeen: Help for the Hurting 141
  It takes a commitment of time to help the hurting.
Chapter Eighteen: Family 149
  The hardest people to share Christ with are your family. Need help?
Chapter Nineteen: Contagious Worship 159
  What does worship have to do with evangelism?
Chapter Twenty: Missed Opportunities 167
  A missed opportunity is a heavy weight to carry.
Chapter Twenty-One: The Journey 173
  It isn't a sprint. It's a journey. Are you ready?
Conclusion: Where Are They Now? 183

Foreword

What a title for a book! Anyone who knows the author personally will appreciate how appropriate it is. He's just a down-and-dirty kind of guy. Don't get me wrong, he's no pagan—he's a sold-out preacher of the gospel. It's just you couldn't tell by looking at him. Nor could you tell it by following him around town. His route is every bit as eclectic as the UPS guy or a bag lady. He is a man who lives real life, with real people, for a divine purpose. He is one of the few I've ever met who actually does evangelism. Again, don't misunderstand—Josh would probably be the last person you'd catch putting a tract under your windshield wiper at the mall or calling cold turkey at someone's door. No, his evangelism looks a lot less like a used-car salesman and much more like an undercover cop. He's an invader who has made himself as comfortable in a homeless camp as at a fellowship dinner. Some of his best friends have piercings in places most of us don't have places. He refuses to flinch when they cuss, offer him a joint, or ask, "Why does God act in such #%@**& ways?" And the beautiful thing is he has nothing to prove to them any more than he does to us.

This book is about real people with real problems encountering a real Savior through Humpty Dumpties like Josh. If you ever thought you could not do evangelism, this book is for you. It is not a list of dos and don'ts; it's not a guilt trip about what you haven't been doing; it's not a theological program with lots of verses to memorize. It is simply a series of stories that open a window on how one life can embody the incarnate Christ for those who need him most.

If you needed to put a theological label on the thesis of this book, it would have to be something like "incarnational evangelism." It is incarnational because Josh marks a path for us to follow in the footsteps of Jesus. It is evangelism because it is good news (that, after all, is the original meaning of the Greek word *euangelion*). For most of us, evangelism is not good news because it scares us to death. The very idea of cold-turkey calling or raving preachers on some soapbox in the market square is intimidating and perhaps even a bit nauseating. We have been duped by the idea that evangelism is about "winning" people to Christ rather than wooing them to the best friend they will ever meet. This sort of evangelism is no less intimidating to the "target," who has a pretty good idea that he or she is about to be snagged into a

Foreword

pyramid scheme or stripped of all earthly pleasures by an archaic Puritanism. I suppose most of us have a sense in the deepest part of our "knower" that there must be a better way. That is what this book is all about.

Final thought: Please don't hear me say this method of evangelism is any less frightening. It is not. What we are dealing with is gut wrenching and terrifying, for you must lay yourself open to the reality of humanity and admit, once and for all, that you too are more familiar with a pig sty than your church clothes would indicate.

> Mark Moore
> Director of the Institute for Christian Resources

Introduction

At what point does it change? There is a point in all of our lives that we decide we don't like getting dirty. As kids there was nothing better than getting dirty. Whether it was playing cars in the dirt pile, making mud pies, or jumping in mud puddles, every kid loves to get dirty. But at some point in our lives it all changes. We avoid stepping in mud puddles and dislike dirt under our fingernails. We do everything we can do to keep from getting dirty.

For many of us this is not only true in our physical lives but also in our spiritual lives. As Christians we avoid getting dirty. We refrain from the dirt of the world. We pride ourselves on the fact that we keep away from dirty sins and dirty people. I wonder what Jesus thinks about this? Is he happy we aren't around sin and sinners, or does it break his heart? I believe many of our churches, pastors, parents, and others teach us to abstain from sin and those who participate in sinful activities, but Jesus taught us very differently. He taught us that we must be around sin and sinful people but to avoid participating in sinful activities.

Now I understand both sides of the coin. As a parent, I want my children to be very careful about how they live and whom they run around with. I don't want them to be influenced by the wrong people. On the other side of the coin, the evangelist (evangelist = one who shares the good news of Christ) in me wants my children to run into the darkness and save people from the fire. So the question becomes: Are we supposed to be in the world where it is dirty? Are we supposed to work with so-called "dirty people"?

Paul made it very clear in 1 Corinthians 5:9–10 how we are supposed to live in this world. There he wrote, "I have written you in my letter not to associate with sexually immoral people—not at all meaning the people of this world who are immoral, or the greedy and swindlers, or idolaters. In that case you would have to leave the world." Through these verses we know we are supposed to live in this world. We are supposed to be actively engaged in the lives of those who are immoral. Paul didn't say not to associate with the above list of sinners. He actually encouraged it but did not condone it.

Too many times I've heard Christians say, "We are in the world, but not of it." Although I agree with that statement, I believe most times it is used in the wrong context. I usually hear someone quoting it and then saying things like: "We aren't supposed to wear that type of clothing"; "You shouldn't go to that movie"; "You can't attend that party"; "You can't do that!" It seems like it is always in the context of "can't." Put it in the context of "can." I can go there because I'm in the world, but I won't participate in the sin. We are in the world, but we are not just here to breathe, take up space, and wait for death or the second coming of Jesus. We are here to live for him, to bring others to him, and to make a difference.

So go places that are dirty…your school, band room, locker room, that party, your living room, etc., and minister to the people who are often called dirty. People get labeled dirty for many different reasons: lifestyle, sin, homelessness, disease, sexual preference, language, financial status, educational status, etc. Both non-Christians and Christians alike label people. We have called them dirty, but God has called them clean. Please open your Bible and read Acts 10:1–48.

In Acts 10, God tells us through the apostle Peter that everyone is labeled "clean" by God. Before the time of Christ people were labeled as Jews or Gentiles. If you were a Jew, you were clean. If you were a Gentile, you were dirty. Jews were not allowed to associate with Gentiles. If a Jew came in contact with a Gentile, the Jew was labeled "unclean." He couldn't go to the temple (the church) and worship God until he had purified himself.

While Jesus was here on earth, he taught his apostles that everyone was worthy of the kingdom of God and that it shouldn't be kept from anyone. He didn't just come for the Jews; he came for all his children. Unfortunately the apostles didn't understand this. Peter got it one day while he was on a roof praying. While praying, he fell into a trance and saw God lowering a sheet from heaven with all kinds of animals on it. He heard God say, "Get up and eat." This happened three different times, but each time he refused, saying, "I have never eaten anything impure or unclean." (Before I continue, understand what Peter was saying. The Jews had a lot of laws they had to follow, and one of them was a very strict law telling them what they could and couldn't eat. God told them exactly what types of animals they were allowed to eat and what types were considered unclean. Peter had always followed that law.) But God replied back to him, "Do not call anything impure that I have made clean."

God was telling Peter, "I'm changing the rules." And then he showed him how by waking him up and sending him on a journey with a bunch of Gentiles. He finished his journey in the house of Cornelius and there he preached to Cornelius and his family. While he was preaching, the Holy Spirit came upon all of them and anointed them. At that moment, Peter understood what was changing. God was officially putting his stamp on the Gentiles and telling Peter, "These people aren't dirty!"

That moment in time opened up the gospel for all people because everyone is clean. Everyone deserves to hear the message of Christ and can freely accept it and be welcomed into heaven. People might label other individuals or groups as dirty, but God doesn't. God sees us for what we can be: clean. Therefore we must take the message of Christ out to those who have been labeled as dirty and let them know God loves them as his children.

As a father I can tell you one of the best smells in the world is my children when they get out of the bathtub. It makes me just want to hold on to them forever. God knows the smell of his children, and he wants to hold each and every one of them forever. He is going to do everything he can to get them back, so you are going to have to make a decision: help him or oppose him.

Peter was questioned when he got back to Jerusalem about why he was preaching to the Gentiles and what happened. He said in Acts 11:15-17, "As I began to speak, the Holy Spirit came on them as he had come on us at the beginning. Then I remembered what the Lord had said: 'John baptized with water, but you will be baptized with the Holy Spirit.' So if God gave them the same gift as he gave us, who believed in the Lord Jesus Christ, who was I to think that I could oppose God?"

I know I don't want to oppose God and stand in his way, therefore I'm going with him, and I'm going to do everything I can to help sinners come to a cleansing relationship with God. He has already made it clear he can clean them. If you want to help people get clean, then you are going to have to be around dirt: body odor, trash, sickness, sin…not that you'll sin, but you will see sin all around you. You must know you'll get dirty, but you'll be helping someone get clean. I know it's all worth it because it's what they need and what God desires.

As you read this book you are going to learn twenty-one life lessons on evangelism. You are going to hear about my encounters with prostitutes, drug addicts, homeless men, orphans, family members, and others. My goal is for you to see from each of my encounters a method or technique I used to share my faith, or what to do or not to do in certain situations. Through the reading of *Get Dirty* your mind is going to be shaped, your heart broken, and your faith stretched. I can tell you my encounters with lost people have changed my life, and I hope they change yours as well. Are you ready to "Get Dirty"?

Chapter One
Dirty Jesus

"Your life should be lived with dirty people, in a dirty church, through a dirty Jesus."

Do not call anything impure that God has made clean.

—Acts 10:15

Love Kids

In January 2003 I went to Haiti for the first time. I had heard about the country and the despair, but those stories did not prepare me for the depth of darkness I saw. It was horrific. Everywhere I looked I saw poverty, despair, and desperation.

I went to Haiti on a mission trip with Compassion International, an organization that ministers to children of poverty. When we first got to Haiti, I asked my team leader what we were going to do on the trip and he said, "Love kids." I told him I knew we were going to love kids, but what else were we going to do? Again, he replied, "Love kids. That is all we are going to do." And that is what we did.

Each day we traveled to different villages and loved kids who were going to school at churches with which Compassion had partnered. It was an awesome experience every time we pulled up to a new project. Hundreds of little Haitian kids would run out to our van and start clapping and cheering. When we got out of the vans, all they wanted was for us to touch them. A handshake, a high-five, a pat on the back, or a hug. Anything that demonstrated our love for them. So I went around hugging a bunch of kids. It felt so good to be used by God through such a simple way.

My last day in Haiti we went to a project where we had another wonderful experience, this time on the island of Lagonav. The island sits right off the shores of Haiti's mainland. It is considered by most the poorest of all of Haiti. We were told there isn't a single drop of fresh water on the entire island. I had never seen such poverty.

When our project visit ended we set out to do a home visit. Home visits were important because they allowed us to see what a child's home life was like, and see how Compassion was helping the child at home. We set out with a young boy. When we got to his home, I couldn't believe what I saw. It was a one-room shack put together with scrap pieces of wood and tin. A total of nine people slept in this one-room home. They invited us to come into the home, but I knew there was no way we could all fit, so I let the other people on my team go in, and I stayed outside by the front door. It was while I was standing there that I noticed her—a little girl in a yellow dress.

The Girl in the Yellow Dress

From a distance I saw a beautiful young girl in a bright yellow dress. As she got closer, though, I started to notice she walked with a limp. A little closer, and her hair was matted together. A little closer, and the look of mental retardation was on her face. A little closer, and I noticed her eyes were crossed. Now the little girl was standing right in front of me, and I could tell the beautiful yellow dress was actually a ripped-up, dirty yellow dress that revealed the right side of the girl's chest. As she stood in front of me, my heart broke. I started praying, "Lord, what do you want me to do for this girl?" And I simply heard him say, "Love her."

Love her? How? I started to think as fast as I could, and I remembered I had a water bottle in my backpack. I know to an American water doesn't seem like an act of love, but in Haiti water is precious. So I grabbed the water bottle and gave it to her. She just looked at it. She had no clue what it was. So I helped her put it up to her mouth and tilted her head back as I gave her a drink. As she was drinking, the water ran all over her face. She laughed loud and had the biggest smile on her face. I held it to her mouth again and got the same result. Water running down her face and laughter. I thought I had done my job, but I heard God say again, "Now love her." So I reached out my hands and put them on her shoulders. I pulled her in a little bit closer and gave her the biggest smile ever. Then I went on my way.

That night as we were sitting around in a circle back at the hotel we all shared stories of our experiences in Haiti. One guy started to share, and as he did, he started crying. He said, "I failed today. I saw a little retarded girl and I failed to minister to her." Then he turned to me and said, "Josh, I want to be like you." Unfortunately I had to stop him very quickly and say, "No, you don't, because I failed today as well." You see, I had heard God say again to me, "Love her," and I knew he meant I should give her a hug. But when I reached out my hands, put them on her shoulders and started to pull her closer to give her a hug, I thought, *I wonder if she has lice?* And with that I stopped. I didn't hug her. What would have happened if I had given that girl a hug or a kiss on the cheek? It might have been the first she had received in years. What would have happened if I had laid my hand on her head and prayed for the Lord to heal her? I'll never know because I was afraid to get dirty!

Does Dirt Bother You?

One thing you will figure out if you want to share your faith is you must be willing to get dirty. There is no way to minister to the lost and hurting of the world if you are afraid of getting your hands a little dirty. Your life should be lived with dirty people, in a dirty church, through a dirty Jesus.

Dirty Jesus

How many non-Christians do you know? How many do you associate with on a regular basis? If every one of your friends is a Christian, then something is wrong. When was the last time you went someplace where you knew there was going to be a lot of dirt (sin)? Why were you there? Were you there to help people find Jesus?

High school students ask me all the time, "Should I go to parties where I know there will be a lot of drinking and sex?" That is a hard question to answer because there are so many variables in it. First, I tell them not to go anywhere where illegal things are happening. That is putting them in a law-breaking situation. Secondly, they have to ask themselves if they are spiritually strong enough. Do they struggle with sexual sin? If so, they shouldn't go to parties where a lot of sexual activity is taking place. But if there isn't anything illegal happening and they are strong enough, then yes, they should go.

You should go to such things because you need to be Jesus there. You need to go to the people and minister to them. You need to get dirty. I get so tired of Christians who hole themselves up in their holy huddles. Good Christian teens have their Christian music, their Christian T-shirts, their Christian friends, and their Christian events. They go to a different church event every night of the week. They become so Christianized they forget about the world around them. It is as if they seek asylum from the world. Jesus never prayed for us to leave the world. He didn't pray we would withdraw from the world. No, he prayed for us to engage the world, to be in the middle of it, and to be the light. He said in John

17:15, "My prayer is not that you take them out of the world but that you protect them from the evil one." Get dirty by being around dirty people.

Second, you need to get dirty by having a dirty church. The church isn't supposed to be a place for people who have it all figured out. It isn't a country club. It is a trauma center. The church should be a place where messed up, dirty people can come to experience God. Your church should be a place where sinners can feel comfortable, not judged. Let's just admit it. We are all a bunch of dirty sinners, so why should we look at people with judging eyes when they enter our church? Are you afraid they are going to make your youth group or your church dirty? Make your youth group and church a place where dirty people are loved. It starts with you always looking at the people who walk through your doors. Immediately go up to them and love them. Shake their hands and hang out with them. Help them meet the Great Physician.

Last, realize Jesus got dirty. Jesus was willing to get dirty to save us. Philippians 2:6–8 says, "Who, being in very nature God, did not consider equality with God something to be grasped, but made himself nothing, taking the very nature of a servant, being made in human likeness. And being found in appearance as a man, he humbled himself and became obedient to death—even death on a cross." Jesus traded in his mansion for a barn full of manure and was born for you. He went from a palace in paradise to a barn in Bethlehem. He got dirty. He didn't say, "They will have to figure this one out on their own." No, he left his throne and traded it in for a cross.

Dirty Jesus

Luke 5 says a man with leprosy fell down on his face behind Jesus and begged him to heal him. Upon hearing this, Jesus reached out his hand, touched the man, and said, "Be clean." By touching this man, Jesus broke the Jewish rules. You weren't allowed to come in contact, let alone touch, a person with leprosy. He became ceremonially unclean and, according to their traditions, couldn't go to the temple and worship God because he was dirty and couldn't be in the presence of God.

Jesus didn't care if he got dirty. What he cared about was that young man. Think about it. Jesus could have simply said, "Be clean." He didn't have to touch him, but he did because he knew the man needed to be loved. I love the depiction of this story in the movie *Matthew* (a movie that walks word by word through the book of Matthew). Jesus doesn't just touch him, but rather gets down on the ground and gives the leper a huge hug. I can only imagine that is what it was probably like. Jesus was, and is, willing to get dirty. Let's follow in his footsteps. Live your life around dirty people, in a dirty church, through the power of a dirty Jesus.

QUESTIONS TO PONDER

What did you learn from the story of the girl in the yellow dress?

When have you failed to minister to someone because you were afraid to get dirty?

Where do you commonly find yourself surrounded by dirty people? How do you minister to them? If you don't ever find yourself around dirty people, where and how could you get around dirty people?

If you were rating yourself, would you say you are on the outside of the world looking in or on the inside of the world looking out? How does God protect you from evil while living inside the world?

What can you do to help your church and youth group be more like a trauma center than a country club?

Scriptures to Study

John 17:14–19
1 Corinthians 5:5–13
Luke 8:40–48 and 8:49–56

Thoughts and Prayers

Spend some time journaling your thoughts about this chapter. What stuck out to you from the stories that were told? How can you implement what you read into your life? And spend some time praying.

Prayer need: _____
Prayer need: _____
Prayer need: _____

Journal

Chapter Two
Be a S.T.A.R.

"The secret is in living a life of evangelism—in living a life every day that focuses on being a S.T.A.R."

He also made the stars.

—Gen. 1:16

A Shattered Dream

I had one goal throughout my entire childhood: I wanted to be a star in the National Football League. I longed to be the best running back in the NFL. Therefore, all the way through elementary school I practiced football. I ate, drank, slept, talked, and studied football. I was the best running back in the pee wee football program in our school system, and I believed that was just the beginning.

Everything was great until seventh grade, when I saw all my dreams come crashing down. I didn't get injured; in fact, I was in perfect health. I was in perfect health because I never got off the bench. I went from being the star of the pee wee football program to being the benchwarmer of the seventh-grade team for one reason: I was short. Everyone else had started growing except me. I was the smallest guy on the team, and because of that, I sat on the bench. The coach didn't give me a chance to show him how I could run the ball. He just looked at my size and made a judgment call. It was at that point that my dreams of being a star were shot down.

I know that seems like a small thing, but at the time it was huge. The only thing I wanted to be was no longer an option, and it crushed me. I thought there was no way for me to ever be a star. Fortunately, I was wrong. I realized I was mistaken one day when I was reading my Bible. I read a passage from the book of Philippians that says, "Become blameless and pure, children of God without fault in a crooked and depraved generation, in which you shine like stars in the universe as you hold out the word of life" (Phil. 2:15–16).

That verse brought about (and still brings about) a pounding in my heart and a vision to my mind. I can be a star. I can be someone who makes a difference. I can be a person whom people look at and say, "Wow." God wants us to go out into the world and to be a star for him. His desire is for us to go out and change the world. He longs for us to be seen. He wants us to be noticed. He wants us to be known, so that we can make him known.

That is what being a S.T.A.R. is all about. People ask me all the time how to share their faith with their friends, family, teammates, etc. The secret is in living a life of evangelism—in living a life every day that focuses on being a S.T.A.R. (Shine, Talk, Action, Reason).

Shine

If you want to bring someone to Christ the first thing you must do is shine. You must "live the life" in front of him or her. Jesus said in Matthew 5:14, "You are the light of the world." He also said in Matthew 5:16, "Let your light shine before men, that they may see your good deeds and praise your Father in heaven." If you will "live the life" in front of non-Christians, they will take notice of your joy, service, love, and compassion and ask you about God.

The problem is most of us haven't figured out how to shine all the time. We are more like lightning bugs. I love lightning bugs, but they drive me crazy because they only give me a glimpse of their light for a second. They are on, off, on, off, just like many of us. How many times do you see yourself or other Christians who are on, off, on, off? The only way for a lightning bug to stay lit is for it to die. Smear it across the pavement and it will shine for a long time. We need to take a lesson from the lightning bug. The only way for us to shine all the time is to die. We must die to ourselves and live for Christ, and by doing so we will reveal Christ to the world. Live a life of goodness, righteousness, and truth, for in this way we will shine. (See Eph. 5:8–9.)

Talk

Living a godly life and shining in front of people is where you start, but if that is all you do, you haven't done enough; all you have done is teach people how to be good. There are a lot of good people in the world who are on their way to hell. I've heard many youth ministers and adults take the easy road and tell people all they have to do is live the life in front of others. "How, then, can they call on the one they have not believed in? And how can they believe in the one whom they have not heard? And how can they hear without someone preaching to them?" (Rom. 10:14).

If you are going to be a S.T.A.R., you must talk. You must open up your mouth at some point and tell people about Christ. When Peter and John were in prison, the Sanhedrin said they would release them as long as they never talked about Jesus again, and they replied, "For we cannot help speaking about what we have seen and heard" (Acts 4:20). Peter and John said there was no way for them not to talk. They had a message in them that had to get out because they had seen God and heard God. They knew they were unable to be quiet. Jeremiah 20:9 says, "But if I say, 'I will not mention him or speak any more in his name, his word is in my heart like a fire, a fire shut up in my bones. I am weary of holding it in; indeed, I cannot.'" It is vital that we recapture that intensity.

To talk doesn't mean you stand on a street corner and shout out Scripture all day. What it means is you look for every opportunity to bring God into your conversations with others. Many times it will be little hints

Be a S.T.A.R.

of God, but by doing that you will be ready when the time is right to challenge someone to think about his or her relationship with God. By talking you become a messenger of God. Revelation 1:18–20 says God holds seven stars in his hand. These stars are the messengers of God…YOU! You are the star in God's hand, so don't ever wonder what you should say or if you have what it takes. Knowing you are in God's hand should give you the confidence you need to be able to talk when called upon.

Action

If you want to be a S.T.A.R. you have to be ready for action. You must be prepared for whom God is going to bring into your life today. First Peter 3:15 says, "Always be prepared to give an answer to everyone who asks you to give the reason for the hope that you have. But do so with gentleness and respect." Every morning you must wake up knowing God is going to bring someone into your life to whom you are going to have the opportunity to witness. It might be a stranger on the street, a lady at a cash register, a teammate, a person on the bus, one of your teachers, or your best friend. If you are not ready for action you will miss this moment in eternity's timeline.

Be ready for action, but remember to do it with gentleness and respect. I've heard students defending their faith by raising their voices and getting irritated. I've seen them get annoyed by the fact that someone would question them on why they do or don't do certain things. I get so mad at Christians who react negatively to such things. If you are being a S.T.A.R., then inevitably you will be asked questions. That is the whole idea. Therefore, make sure when you answer people you do so with gentleness and respect. Don't be mean. Don't raise your voice. Don't make them feel ignorant. Realize they are non-Christians, and this is your open door to talk to them.

Reason

The reason you evangelize people is if you don't, they will burn in hell. I'm aware that wasn't said in a soft, gentle way. But, it was spoken in truth. There are people you come in contact with every day who are on the road to hell. It is your job to save them. Jude 23 says, "Snatch others from the fire and save them." God has entrusted his people to rescue sinners from the fires of hell. You need to realize it is your duty to reach out to everyone, no matter what the person is like, because you shouldn't want anyone to burn. Your heart needs to hurt for everyone: friends, family, rich, poor, tattooed, homeless, enemies, sick, minorities, those on your street, and those halfway around the world. Hell is real, and you need to save people from it. You can't ever let this leave your mind. If you forget the reason behind why you need to bring people to Jesus, then you will stop doing it. You will no longer be burdened for their souls. You will no longer be willing to live the life in front of them. You'll neglect talking about Christ when doors are open. You will forget to take advantage of opportunities for evangelism. That is why it is such a burden on my heart that you never forget the reason why you should be a S.T.A.R. I plead with you, with tears in my eyes, to remember the reason. The reason is to save people from the fire.

My seventh-grade coach told me I would never be a star. He was wrong. The Creator of the universe has called me to be one. In addition, he has called you to be one as well. So don't hold back, don't be hidden, don't burn out. No, take your place and be the star God has called you to be. Be a S.T.A.R.

Questions to Ponder

When was there a time that you got your dreams shot down?

What sins do you need to "die to" that are keeping you from shining?

When was the last time you talked about Christ to someone?

Whom can you talk to today about Christ? Pray to be ready for action.

List five people by name whom you want to save from hell.

What is it going to take for you to be a S.T.A.R.?

Scriptures to Study

Matthew 13:36–43
2 Corinthians 4:1–6
Ephesians 4:29–5:2
Luke 16:19–31

Thoughts and Prayers

Spend some time journaling your thoughts about this chapter. What stuck out to you from the stories? How can you implement what you read into your life? When you're finished journaling, take some time to pray.

Prayer need: _____
Prayer need: _____
Prayer need: _____

Journal

_____

_____

Chapter Three
Do You See Anything?

"Look up when you walk."

Jesus asked, "Do you see anything?"
—Mark 8:23

Ybor City

As I was speaking in Tampa, Florida, at a youth convention, I kept hearing the students talk about Ybor City. I asked them what it was, and they said, "A place that you wouldn't want to go. It is a place where a ton of people go to sin." They didn't know me very well, because that is exactly the type of place I enjoy going.

When the event was over that night, I went and got a bite to eat and then headed for Ybor City. Cars are not allowed into the town center at night, so I parked in a nearby parking lot and started walking toward the middle of the action. I was blown away by what I saw. I quickly noticed the streets were lined with bars, strip joints, black magic shops, body art studios, dance clubs, and other establishments where sin happens. There were tons of people in these businesses and shops but even more just hanging out on the streets, some walking, some talking, some drinking, and some singing. I knew right away it was going to be a great night. What I later came to understand was that it was more than just a great night. It was a night where Jesus broke me, called me, and changed me.

The first person I encountered was a young homeless boy. I'm guessing he was about fourteen years old. His face was dirty and his hair was all matted together. He asked me what I was doing in Ybor, and I just said, "Hanging out and looking for some people to talk to." He hung out with me for a while and then went on his way. I saw him three or four more times that night, and every time he would hang out with me for about five minutes. It was very obvious he was looking for someone who would love him.

The next encounter I had was with two young guys. I started talking with them and asked them why they come to Ybor. They replied, "We're here to get something." I asked them what they were trying to get, and they replied, "Girls, drugs, alcohol, or trouble. We don't really care what it is as long as we get something." We talked for a little while after that, and then they went looking to "get something."

My last encounter of the night was with a young lady. She was standing in front of a strip joint trying to drum up some business. She stood there, and as guys walked by she hit on them and struck up a conversation. Then she tried to convince them to go inside and let her dance for them.

When I saw this young girl, my heart went out to her so I started walking toward her. In her mind she saw business coming, so she approached me as well. We talked for a while, and then she asked if I wanted to go inside. I politely let her know I wasn't interested in going inside but would love to continue our conversation. As the conversation continued I asked her in a very non-judgmental way, "Why do you dance for people?"

Her reply broke my heart. "I have a three-year-old daughter and a bad habit, and I must support them both."

The conversation ended by my telling her I loved her and I would pray for her daughter and her addiction.

From there I stood in the middle of an intersection and looked down the road at the mass of people. I started praying for the people I saw, and I asked God to open my eyes and allow me to see them as he does. Immediately, my heart started to break. The pain hit my heart, the thoughts went to my head, and the tears came to my eyes. It was at that moment that God started to open my eyes. It was as if I started seeing people the way he did, as lost people who had no hope. He brought Luke 19:41–42 to my mind: "As he approached Jerusalem and saw the city, he wept over it and said, 'If you, even you, had only known on this day what would bring you peace.'" In the middle of a road in Ybor City, the Lord opened my eyes.

Open Your Eyes

You see things all the time that you choose to ignore. Have you seen the speed limit signs? Yet, you still speed. Have you seen the sign at the top of the rollercoaster that says, "Keep your hands inside the car?" Yet, you still raise your hands. You see lost people every day, but do you really see them? Have you opened your eyes to them?

In Luke 7:11–13 we see Jesus' eyes were open to those around him. In the story Jesus was walking into town with a crowd following him. As he was walking, a funeral procession was leaving town. If you can imagine, everyone in Jesus' crowd was probably throwing a party because they were with him, yet just on the other side of the road was a crowd in mourning. I wonder how many people in Jesus' crowd even noticed the funeral?

Jesus not only noticed the procession, he also noticed the widow. It says in verse 13, "When the Lord saw her, his heart went out to her." Jesus' eyes were open. We need to have the eyes of Christ. We need to look around and see people who are lost, who are spiritually dead, and who need him. In the movie *The Sixth Sense*, the lead character says he sees dead people everywhere. What do you see? If you see lost people, it will break your heart.

Notice it says in verse 13 when Jesus saw her, his heart went out to her. I can promise you when you open your eyes what you will see will break your heart. It is an unfortunate, yet necessary, thing. Unfortunate because it will make your heart hurt, but necessary because it pushes you to do something.

One day I was walking through Atlanta when I saw a homeless man in a wheelchair. I couldn't stop crying.

I said under my breath, "Quit crying and get over it." I didn't think anyone heard me, but the guy I was walking with turned and rebuked me and said, "You prayed that your eyes would be open. You'll be crying for the rest of your life." He put me in my place and I'm glad he did. I hope I never stop crying, because if I do then that means I've stopped seeing lost people and hurting for them.

Eyes Up

Let me encourage you to keep your eyes up as well as open. Look up when you walk. Look around when you are just hanging out. Many people miss seeing lost people because they look down at the ground all the time. Watch people walk and you will notice they look down most of the time…you do the same thing. Start walking with your eyes up, because by doing so it will open opportunities for you to converse with people. People ask me all the time how I meet so many people and engage in conversations with them. I always tell them it is because I walk with my eyes up. It is a very simple thing, but trust me, it works.

QUESTIONS TO PONDER

What did you learn from the night in Ybor City?

Are your eyes currently shut or open? What will it take for you to open them? What will it take for you to keep them open all the time?

When was the last time your heart broke because you saw a lost person?

Do you walk with your eyes up or do you look at the ground? Give it a test and see what happens.

Scriptures to Study

John 4:34–36
2 Corinthians 4:18
Matthew 6:22–23
Matthew 13:15–17

Thoughts and Prayers

Spend some time journaling your thoughts about this chapter. What stuck out to you from the stories? How can you implement what you read into your life? Spend some time praying.

Prayer need: _____
Prayer need: _____
Prayer need: _____

Journal

_____

_____

Chapter Four

Hell

"Stand up and fight with everything you have because life without God leads to suffering, separation, and sorrow, but life with God leads to healing, hope, and heaven."

Snatch others from the fire and save them.
—Jude 23

Kristie

I found myself in the weirdest place ever, trying to minister to people. I was in New Orleans graveyards. These old graveyards have aboveground tombs and history all over them. The graveyard I was in actually had been featured in several movies and is a major tourist attraction in the city. The place gave off a weird aura, because you knew everyone walking around was a tourist, but each was still being quiet and reverent because it was a graveyard. It was a perfect place for me to be, because at the time I was trying to interview people about the subject of death and the afterlife.

I had talked to a lot of people throughout the day. Each person broke my heart because I kept hearing people say they didn't believe in God or in such a thing as an afterlife. My heart broke for these people because I knew they had no hope. Everyone's story was the same, except for Kristie's.

Kristie was a young college girl who stopped to talk to me. We shot the breeze for a little while, and then I started asking her more direct questions. She had a friend with her who endured our conversation but wouldn't participate in it. I eventually asked Kristie how she felt about dying. The tone in her voice changed drastically and was laced with fear when she said, "I don't like to think about it because it scares me."

I asked her to explain, and she said, "I'm afraid of where I'll go after death. I was raised in a church and I know the way I'm living right now isn't in line with what I was taught."

I then asked her, "So you believe in hell?"

As the tears started to well up in her eyes, she said, "Yeah, and I'm afraid that is where I'm going to go after I die."

When Kristie said that my heart broke. The last thing you want to hear is someone who believes in hell knows she is on her way there. I started to share Jesus with Kristie and explain that he could save her, but her friend had heard enough. Her friend said in an irritated voice, "Come on, Kristie, we've heard enough from this guy." Then her friend grabbed her hand and started pulling her down the road. I tried to continue the conversation, but her friend won. She was gone!

Hell Is Real

To this day I can remember what Kristie looks like. I can remember her hair, her clothes, her tear-filled eyes, and most importantly her heart. My memories of her hurt because on that day I lost the battle. I was in the middle of a battle with Satan that day and he won. I remember the feeling I had that day. I remember feeling as if Satan raised his ugly head and while I was trying to share the gospel in the middle of a graveyard he said, "No, not today. She's mine."

I can't stand losing. I'm a competitor and a winner. Losing isn't something I take lightly, especially when the battle is a spiritual battle for a soul. Satan ticked me off that day because he was able to keep someone in bondage, in chains.

Hell is real. The Bible teaches us that. Kristie believed that. And because of that truth, we have to free people from it. Jude 23 says, "Snatch people from the fire and save them." Isaiah 61:1 says, "To proclaim freedom for the captives, and release from darkness for the prisoners." Hell holds people captive through extreme suffering, separation, and sorrow. These three characteristics of hell can be seen as you read the story of the rich man and Lazarus in Luke 16:19–26:

> There was a rich man who was dressed in purple and fine linen and lived in luxury every day. At his gate was laid a beggar named Lazarus, covered with sores

and longing to eat what fell from the rich man's table. Even the dogs came and licked his sores. The time came when the beggar died and the angels carried him to Abraham's side. The rich man also died and was buried. In hell, where he was in torment, he looked up and saw Abraham far away, with Lazarus by his side. So he called to him, "Father Abraham, have pity on me and send Lazarus to dip the tip of his finger in water and cool my tongue, because I am in agony in this fire." But Abraham replied, "Son, remember that in your lifetime you received your good things, while Lazarus received bad things, but now he is comforted here and you are in agony. And besides all this, between us and you a great chasm has been fixed, so that those who want to go from here to you cannot, nor can anyone cross over from there to us."

This story shows us that hell sucks. It is a place of extreme suffering. Look at the rich man's words. He was in extreme pain, agony, and suffering. He longed for a drink of cold water. He was burning. Hell is defined as the lake of fire (Rev. 20:14) and as a place of weeping and gnashing/grinding of teeth (Matt. 8:12). Hell is a place of fire. A place where the fire never dies out but keeps burning and burning. The pain never decreases or increases. It is extreme from the beginning and forever.

This story also shows us that hell is a place of separation. Notice Abraham said a "chasm," a canyon, had been fixed so no one can go between heaven and hell. This is an important thing to realize. Some people would say hell is a place of punishment, and once you have served your sentence you get released. Scripture teaches us there is one judgment. Once you have been sent to hell you are there forever. It isn't temporary. It is a life sentence, an eternity of separation from God. That is hard for us to fathom because even though God is in heaven and we are on earth, we still aren't separated from him. His presence is here. In hell it is total separation from God. Separation from anything that is good, because he is the giver of all good gifts. Thus, if it's good, it ain't there!

This story also teaches us that hell is a place of extreme sorrow. I think the worst thing about hell is that you will have your memory. Abraham said to the rich man, "Remember." Think about that for a second. If you can remember, that means you will be able to remember all the good things you had in life, the comfort of your house, the beauty of sleep, the coolness of water, etc. You also will be able to remember the opportunities you had to accept Jesus. Think about the people who are currently in hell, remembering they could have saved themselves from the fire by accepting Christ: Pilate could have accepted Christ, Judas could have accepted Christ, and your friend or family member who heard the gospel preached at church or through you could have accepted Christ. They will remember the day they said, "No thanks." Because of that they are paying the penalty.

Hell is a very real place and we must save people from it. I'm often reminded of Kristie and the battle I lost with her that day. I can't stand losing because I know every time I lose, a soul loses as well. Stand up and fight with everything you have because life without God leads to suffering, separation, and sorrow. But life with God leads to healing, hope, and heaven.

QUESTIONS TO PONDER

What did you learn from Kristie's story?

Are you afraid of dying?

Have you ever battled with Satan? When? What was the outcome? How did it make you feel?

In your own words, how would you describe hell to someone?

Prepare yourself for battle by spending some time in silence with God and praying for people specifically by name.

Scriptures to Study

Matthew 18:7–9
Revelation 20:7–15
Matthew 10:27–28

Thoughts and Prayers

Spend some time journaling your thoughts about this chapter. What stuck out to you from the stories? How can you implement what you read into your life? Spend some time praying.

Prayer need: _____
Prayer need: _____
Prayer need: _____

Journal

_____

_____

Chapter Five

Gravity

"My heart could take no more."

Jesus wept.

—John 11:35

Life on Bourbon Street

Bourbon Street in New Orleans is a place of beauty, history, big churches, old streets, great music, and a lot of sin. People go there to fulfill their appetites for evil, the world, and sin. It is famous for Mardi Gras, which takes all of the sin to a completely different level. But even when Mardi Gras isn't taking place you still will find all-night parties, beads for revealing your breasts, black magic/voodoo shops, live sex shows, and people everywhere drinking Pat O'Brien's famous hurricanes. It is a place where Satan is stirring up a party, telling lies, and devouring people. It is also a city where you will find broken people with broken hearts who are looking for love.

It was early on a Friday evening when I first strolled down Bourbon Street. As soon as I walked onto the street I felt the weight of the spiritual darkness. I could feel the gravity of the situation I was walking into. It felt like I was walking into a dark, hazy, abandoned house. I could sense from the feeling in my heart that I was going to be encountering a lot of people that night who needed Jesus. I knew that night I would be a bright light shining in a dark, dark world. I knew I was walking in the enemy's territory. It was a place that desperately needed the light of Christ. I met several people that night, all from different places with different stories.

Here are a few short stories of my encounters.

Bea

Bea was my first real encounter of the evening. Bea was an older lady, probably around fifty, and was totally blitzed. She was so drunk she could hardly stand up. She caught my eye because of what she was wearing. She had a big blue, yellow, and green feather boa wrapped around her neck that matched the mask she was wearing, a traditional Mardi Gras mask decorated with feathers. The mask disguised her nose and eyes. It also covered the real Bea.

I started walking in her direction, hoping a conversation would occur, and it did. She looked up through the holes in her mask and greeted me. I said hello and asked her how she was doing.

She replied, "Oh, I'm great. I flew into town yesterday and have been drinking nonstop since then."

At this point she threw her arm around me and in the process spilled her drink all down the front of my shirt. We continued to talk for a while. As I was finishing up the conversation I said, "Well, Bea, I hope you have a good night and I want you to know I love you and Jesus loves you."

With those words her demeanor completely changed. It was as if you could spiritually see the mask coming off of her face. The Mardi Gras mask was still in place, but now I was looking at the true Bea. I saw her through her eyes. She started crying and softly said, "I need help. My life is falling apart. My marriage is on the rocks. I live in sin daily, and I need Jesus to forgive me."

Bea allowed her mask to come off. We all have worn masks before, haven't we? In Mark 10:17–22, the rich young ruler had a mask on as well. The young man ran up to Jesus and fell on his knees and asked him what he had to do to inherit eternal life. Jesus responded by telling him to keep the law. The young man said he had done that since he was a boy.

Now, stop for a second and picture this encounter. Here is a young man of great wealth and pride. It doesn't come right out and say in the text he was prideful, but we can assume that because of the way Jesus responded when the young man called him good and because he said, "These I have kept since I was a boy." Can you see the young man's face as he says those words? Can you see the mask on his face?

I love what it says in verse 21: "Jesus looked at him and loved him." Jesus wasn't disgusted by his response. He didn't rebuke him. He loved him and then responded to him by saying, "One thing you lack. Go and sell everything you have...then come follow me." In verse 22 it says, "At this the man's face fell." His mask came off. But rather than embrace the words spoken to him, he rejected them. He looked Jesus square in the eye and said no by his actions. How sad that day must have been!

I'll never forget Bea and the mask she wore. I'll never forget how the simple, yet powerful, words "I love you" changed her that day and helped her remove the mask.

Melissa

Melissa was an eighteen-year-old girl who was living the life of a gypsy. Gypsies are people who travel from place to place because they either don't want to plant roots or they don't have a home. Melissa had a home until her eighteenth birthday. On her birthday Melissa told her mom she was tired of her Minnesota town and life, and she took off. She hopped on a freight train and rode it for a while. From that train she caught another, and another, and another. She spent her days hitchhiking by railroad, not knowing where the train would take her. Melissa's only hope was it would take her somewhere other than the little town in Minnesota where she grew up.

Gravity

Her latest stop was New Orleans. When I saw her, she was standing on a street corner with a couple of guys she had met on the tracks. We talked for a while on the street, and then we met again outside of an ice-cream parlor. She was sitting by herself, so I asked her if she wanted to go in and get some ice-cream with my friend and me. She replied she didn't have any money. I assured her we wouldn't let that stand in the way. So she went in with us. Over great ice-cream we enjoyed a deep discussion about home. I encouraged her to remember her roots and start catching trains headed north.

I wonder how many people need to take the next train home. How many people are just like Melissa? How many are just like the lost son? In Luke 15:11–20, there is a familiar story about a son who left home. The son left home looking for bigger and better things. He left looking for excitement in life, just like Melissa did. He ended up spending every dime he had on wild living, and eventually living in a pigpen, eating with the animals. I know I've been there. How about you? Have you left home looking for better things? Maybe not literally, but have you, or your friends, spiritually left God?

Remember, God is waiting for you to return. He longs for all of his children to come home, no matter what they have done. In the parable Jesus told, the young man came to his senses one day and headed for home. His father came out to meet him. In Luke 15:20 it says, "But while he was still a long way off, his father saw him and was filled with compassion for him; he ran to his son, threw his arms around him and kissed him." Therefore, make sure you turn toward home and help others to do the same. When you take one step toward home, he will take the rest of them.

Lucas

Lucas was the typical guy most people would avoid. He was dressed in all black: black pants, black shirt, and black trench coat. He was covered with piercings all over his ears and face. I got into a conversation with him because there was a guy standing in the middle of the street across from us with a huge sign that read, "Hell Is Forever." I knew the sign was true, but I knew the guy who was holding it with his judgmental attitude was doing nothing. All he was doing was ticking Lucas off. And to be honest, he was ticking me off as well. In my opinion, that type of evangelism just pushes people away from God. Where is the compassion? Where is the mercy? Where is the relationship? Yes, hell is forever, and we need to be burdened by that, but there are better ways to tell people about Christ.

Lucas and I fell into a deep discussion about religion. At the beginning of the conversation, he had no clue I was a believer because I sided with him about most of his opinions. I agreed with him that religion separates and divides. I also agreed with him that most religions are fake. But what really floored him was when I agreed with him that Jesus is a crutch. He said people believe in Jesus just because they need a crutch. I totally agreed with him on that and said, "That is exactly why I need Jesus, because I need help getting to heaven."

Don't get upset if someone tells you that you only believe in Christ because you need a crutch. It's true.

You need him. You can't get there on your own. And there is no other person to whom you can turn for the answers.

John 6 says many of the disciples deserted Jesus because of his hard teachings. Because of this, he asked the apostles if they wanted to leave as well. Peter responded by saying, "Lord, to whom shall we go? You have the words of eternal life" (John 6:68). Jesus has the words of eternal life and I need them.

My response took him by surprise because I didn't disagree and argue with him. Instead, I agreed with him, not in a negative way, but in a positive manner. That simple conversation did more for his faith in God than a sign reading "Hell Is Forever" ever will.

The Weight of My Walk

I talked to several more people that night until finally I was spiritually exhausted. My last encounter of the evening was with two young ladies. They quickly turned on me and started cursing at me because of my faith. At that, I was done. My heart could take no more. I went to the side of the road, sat down, and started weeping. For the remainder of the night I was spiritually overwhelmed. My heart was bleeding, and my soul felt the weight of all the lost people I met that night. I can't totally explain what was going on, but I can tell you I was done. I had been poured out, and I needed to be refreshed by the Lord.

The feeling I experienced that night reminded me of the way Christ must have felt in the Garden of Gethsemane. I know the situation was extremely different, but the spiritual weight of it all was of the same genre. Luke 22 says when Jesus went to the garden, he prayed with such intensity that his sweat was like drops of blood falling to the ground. He was in such agony over the situation that he was actually bleeding.

In the midst of the garden, an angel showed up. The angel was sent by the Father with words to strengthen and encourage Jesus. I believe the angel most likely said two main things that night: his Dad loved him, and he needed to complete the task. When God talks to us, he usually says words of comfort or words of conviction. I believe that night he gave Jesus words of comfort for the situation ahead. I also think he spoke words of conviction because Jesus didn't sway from the job ahead of him. He stayed the course. Even though it was extremely difficult, painful, and heartbreaking, he didn't quit.

That night on Bourbon Street I wanted to quit. My heart hurt too much, and I was ready to give up. Yet that wasn't what God called me to do. He called me to get some rest and to get back at it. The next day I found myself right back on Bourbon Street, trying to be a light to help people get out of the darkness. I can tell you if you want to be an evangelist, if you truly desire to use your life to tell people about Christ, get ready for the weight of it all. Be prepared for the pain, the heartache, the rejections, and the tears. There will be days when it seems too much to bear. When those days hit, think of Jesus in the garden. Remember the Father wants to comfort you by telling you that you are his child. He also will convict you by telling you to get up and go into the world. When you accept the task of evangelism, you

Gravity

are putting the weight of people's souls on your back. It is a heavy weight, but one worth carrying.

I finished this chapter right before Hurricane Katrina wreaked havoc on the city of New Orleans. As I saw the news reports, my heart was breaking because I knew the people in this chapter and many others I met on Bourbon Street were fighting for their lives. They had no home to protect, but also had no transportation to get them out of the city. When you think of New Orleans and Hurricane Katrina, don't forget about people like Bea, Melissa, and Lucas.

Questions to Ponder

What did you learn from Bea's story? What mask do you hide behind?

What did you learn from Melissa's story? Have you turned toward home?

What did you learn from Lucas's story? Is Jesus your crutch? If so, how would you explain that to people?

What did you learn from the story of Jesus in the garden? Read Luke 22:39–46.

Do you understand "the weight of people's souls"? Have you felt it before? Are you willing to accept it?

Scriptures to Study

Romans 7:24–25
Luke 15:11–24
Acts 4:12
Luke 22:39–46
Isaiah 53:4–6

Thoughts and Prayers

Spend some time journaling your thoughts about this chapter. What stuck out to you from the stories? How can you implement what you read into your life? When you are finished journaling, take some time to pray.

Prayer need: _____
Prayer need: _____
Prayer need: _____

Journal

_____

_____

Chapter Six
Opportunity Knocks

"Money I don't have for you tonight, but what I do have is Jesus, and if you want some of that, then let's talk."

Therefore, as we have opportunity, let us do good to all people.

—Gal. 6:10

The Rickster

It was a night on the streets in downtown Palm Springs, California. I was ready to do God's will and share my faith, but what unfolded was a life-changing appointment. I had been speaking at the Palm Springs Convention Center at a high school conference. When the conference ended for the night, the students all went into discussion groups. I, on the other hand, went to find something to eat. I had never been to Palm Springs, but I figured there had to be a main drag. I found it, and I was in heaven. Main Street itself was closed, but vendors were lined up and down the road. People were everywhere, and I immediately knew God was going to give me an opportunity to share my faith that night. I started walking with my eyes up and praying that God would bring someone into my path whom I could share with. As I walked I saw a Mexican cantina and thought, *I'll go in there and get some food and surely God will bring someone into my path.*

As I got close to the door he put someone in front of me, but I didn't want to take the time to minister to him. You see, he was a homeless man standing on the side of the road begging for money. I remember specifically saying to myself, "Lord, don't let this guy ask me for money. I don't have time for him tonight. There are people you want me to go and talk to about you."

Well, sure enough, the man stopped me and asked me for money. I gave him a response I don't normally give. I said back to him, "Money I don't have for you tonight, but what I do have is Jesus, and if you want some of that, then let's talk."

I thought for sure he'd say no and that would free me up to go find someone to minister to. "Let's talk," he responded, and my jaw hit the ground.

He told me his name was Rick, but he went by "The Rickster." I ended up talking with him for a long time about his life, his faith, and Jesus. After a while he asked me if it was all right if while we talked he still asked people for money, because "he had to make a living."

Opportunity Knocks 57

"Fine by me" I said as we carried on our conversation.

What I began to see broke my heart. Because of where I was standing, people assumed there were two homeless men, not one. I saw their faces: faces of disgust, faces of mistrust, faces of "get a job," and faces of rejection. As I stood there I realized what he saw every day from people—those who ignored, rejected, and downgraded him with every look. I decided right then and there that I would never pass a homeless man again without at least smiling and saying hello.

We continued to talk for a while. He asked me what I was doing in town and I told him about the youth conference. He acted very interested so I invited him to attend with me the next night. He was excited I asked and said he would love to go, so I told him I would pick him up at six o'clock the next night right at that spot.

I showed up the next night in my rental car to pick him up. It was a brand-new Mustang convertible. When he looked at the car, he just smiled and hopped in. We cruised around town a little while, and he filled me in on the good and the bad of the city, and then we made it to the conference. The worship was great that night. Once the band was done playing I got up on stage and preached. What took place next was amazing.

When I was finished preaching we had a time of ministry—a time where I encouraged people to accept Christ as their Savior, a time to come up front and pray, and a time to go and minister to people if God had placed someone on your heart. While this was happening I noticed a young boy go back and start talking to Rick.

Then another one, and another, and another. Eventually there were probably eight to ten kids hanging around with Rick, talking to him and praying for him. It was amazing to see these students ministering to him.

As we were driving back into the city I asked Rick if he enjoyed the night. He looked at me as if he were a kid on Christmas morning. He had the biggest smile on his face and a tear in his eye. He showed me a Bible a kid had given him. He couldn't even talk, he was so excited. And, in addition to all of that, he accepted Christ as his Savior that night. It was an amazing night!

A Divine Appointment

How many times do we miss things because we aren't tuned in to God? The night before I almost missed an appointment God had ordained for me. When I saw Rick I wanted nothing to do with him. If anything, I saw him as a roadblock, a detour to an appointment God had for me with someone in the Mexican cantina. I was so focused on my thoughts that I almost missed God's.

We must realize God has appointments for us that we don't even know about. Think about Peter and John. In Acts 3, it says they were on their way to the temple to pray. As they were on their way they passed by a man who was begging for money. When asked for money, Peter said, "Silver or gold I do not have, but what I have I give you. In the name of Jesus Christ of Nazareth, walk."

Peter and John were going to the temple to pray, not to heal someone and tell him about Jesus. But when given the opportunity to tell this man about Christ,

Opportunity Knocks

they did. They recognized a divine appointment and seized it.

God is going to put divine appointments in front of you. You must seize them. Seize them on the field, in the hallway, and at the gas station.

If you want to seize these divine moments, you must be flexible. Slow down, leave your agenda behind, and be flexible. When you are rushed, it is almost impossible, so slow down and get rid of some of the commotion in your life. We must be willing to be flexible and go wherever his will leads us. I'm not saying to always fly by the seat of your pants, but I am saying to be flexible. Be open-minded to appointments God has ordained for you that you don't even know about.

QUESTIONS TO PONDER

What did you learn from the story about Rick?

When was the last time you seized a divine appointment?

Can you remember passing up an appointment? How does that make you feel?

What can you do to slow down your life to allow for more flexibility?

Make sure you pray about God sending you some appointments.

Scriptures to Study

Acts 3:1–10
Ephesians 5:15–16
Colossians 4:5–6
Ephesians 6:19–20

Thoughts and Prayers

Spend some time journaling your thoughts about this chapter. What stuck out to you from the stories? How can you implement what you read into your life? Spend some time praying.

Prayer need: _____
Prayer need: _____
Prayer need: _____

Journal

_____

_____

Chapter Seven
I Love Sinners

"I no longer look at their current lifestyle or sin, I look at their soul."

Above all, love each other deeply, because love covers over a multitude of sins.

—1 Peter 4:8

Alice

I don't know who benefited more from our conversation, Alice or me. Alice was a lady I met on Bourbon Street in New Orleans. She was a middle-aged homeless woman who had a skin disease that was causing her hands and face to break out with bumps. Alice wore dark jeans and a dirty black shirt that matched her dark, uncombed hair. As I was walking down the street, she and her boyfriend came up to me and asked me for a dollar so they could buy a beer. I gave a dollar to her boyfriend and said, "I'll give you a dollar, you go get a drink, and I'll stay here and talk to Alice."

While he was gone, Alice and I had a great conversation. We talked about where she was from, where she was going, her favorite city, etc. Basically we were just making small talk. When her boyfriend got back, we talked for a little while longer and then I said goodbye. I could tell in my spirit I was going to have other chances to talk with Alice and Travis.

And that I did. I ran into Alice and Travis two more times that night. Each time we would just shoot the breeze for a little while. They would stop and tell me about their adventures in the city. With each conversation, I felt our friendship grow, and I knew God was paving a path for ministry.

A Bathroom and a Window Seal

The appointment for true ministry took place the next night. I was in an ice-cream shop just off of Bourbon Street, sharing an ice-cream cone with one of my friends and a runaway named Melissa (see chapter 5). Alice came walking in very fast. When she saw me, she came up to me and said, "I'm glad to see you. Do you know where a bathroom is?"

No sooner did she get the words out when the manager of the small shop came up behind her, grabbed her by the shoulder, and said, "Get out of my store! We don't allow beggars in here."

Immediately, I saw Alice's face fall. I quickly told the manager Alice was my friend and she wasn't in there begging, but the damage was already done. The judgment had been cast and Alice's heart was crushed. With sadness on her face, she asked me again where a bathroom was, so I pointed her toward a place just down the street.

When I left the ice-cream shop I ran into Alice one more time. She and Travis were sitting on a window ledge. We talked as usual, and then the moment I had been waiting for happened. She looked at me and said, "I've got to ask you something. What type of minister buys a homeless woman a beer?"

I moved into her space a little, looked straight into her eyes, and simply replied, "Alice, the type of minister that loves you and wants you to know that God loves you."

With that she stretched out her dirty hands, grabbed hold of my head, pulled me in closer, and planted a very polite kiss on my cheek. Then she simply said, "Thank you for loving me and giving me God's love."

A Friend of Sinners

If you want to bring people to Christ you must be willing to love sinners. Alice's story can teach you two very valuable lessons about loving sinners and ministering to them. You must come to an understanding of the spiritual state of non-Christians.

I get asked all the time, "Don't you think it was wrong that you bought Alice a beer?" I must answer this a couple of different ways. One, realize I didn't do anything illegal. Alice is a middle-aged woman who, by our laws, is old enough to consume alcohol. If it had been illegal, I would have said no to her. Is it wrong for a forty-year-old to drink? This is highly debated in many of our churches, but you need to understand something regardless of whether you think drinking is right or wrong: Alice wasn't a Christian. Alice didn't belong to the church, the body of Christ. She was a nonbeliever. Therefore if she wanted to get totally blitzed, what does it really matter?

This is where it is crucial for you to understand the spiritual state of a non-Christian. If a person has never asked Jesus to forgive him or her of sin, then what does it really matter to sin a little more?

Which sin sends you to hell? The first one you commit. You don't get sent to hell once your sins have piled up to a certain height, nor do you get sent to a deeper level of hell the more you sin. It is when you sin for the very first time that you are separated from God. It is at that point that you need Jesus as your Savior. Alice had sinned long before I met her.

Understanding the spiritual state of the non-Christian will help you to reach out to people to whom you normally wouldn't extend love. Many times people won't reach out to others because they say things like, "That person uses drugs all the time" or "That person spread a rumor about me" or "That person is living an alternative lifestyle." Who cares if they are using drugs, selling drugs, having sex, telling lies, etc.? Now, don't get me wrong, I don't want teenagers to be doing those things, because I know physically it can kill them. But

I Love Sinners

spiritually speaking, it is when they lied to their mom or disobeyed their dad that they actually sent their souls down a path to hell.

Another reason many Christians won't minister to those living in sin is because they are afraid of guilt by association. They don't want people thinking they are involved in the same things. I'm glad Jesus didn't care what others thought. In Luke 5, Jesus called Levi, the tax collector, to follow him. Immediately, Levi left everything and followed him.

Shortly after that, Levi threw a huge banquet for Jesus. Levi invited all his friends...all of the other tax collectors, misfits, and undesirables of the town. Word got out to the Pharisees and they questioned Jesus' disciples, saying, "Why do you eat and drink with tax collectors and sinners?"

Jesus responded by saying, "It is not the healthy who need a doctor, but the sick. I have not come to call the righteous, but sinners to repentance" (Luke 2:30–32). Because Jesus was hanging out with sinners they called him a sinner, but he didn't care what people said because he knew the truth and his calling. He was called to hang out with the lost and sick of the world.

We must be willing to hang out with the lost and the sick as well. It doesn't mean you always have to hang out at their parties, but it does mean you have to be willing to associate with them when it is appropriate. Therefore, don't look at their current lifestyles or sins. Look at their hearts and realize they are sick and need a doctor.

The second thing you can learn from Alice's story is the words "I love you" are very powerful. I constantly tell non-Christians I love them. All people long to be loved, therefore I want people to know I love them. I purposely say, "I love you and God loves you." I state it in that order because people are accustomed to others saying, "God loves you" or "God bless you." But it takes on a whole new meaning when you are willing to declare, "I love you." I believe by professing my personal love for them I have earned the right to then tell them my God loves them as well.

Think about Jesus for a second. He exemplified this truth not by just stating that God, his Father, loves us, but by demonstrating it through actions. His actions showed people they were loved. His words reaffirmed his love. Because of his actions and his words, he was able to not only love people but also connect them to his Father. Jesus' whole purpose in life was to connect people to God. He did it by first loving them himself. It wasn't enough for God to just say he loved us. He went the next step and proved it by giving us his Son. When his Son was here on earth, he connected people to his Father by loving them with actions and words first, so that secondly he could show them how much God loved them.

QUESTIONS TO PONDER

What did you learn from Alice's story?

Explain how you think Alice felt in the ice-cream shop, both her negative and positive feelings.

When have you missed opportunities to minister to people because you let their sins get in the way?

I Love Sinners

How do you minister to someone who is entangled in sin and yet stay out of sin yourself?

When was the last time you told a non-Christian you loved him or her?

Scriptures to Study

John 15:9–17
Romans 5:6–8
1 Corinthians 13:1–13
2 Corinthians 5:18–21
1 John 3:16–18

Thoughts and Prayers

Spend some time journaling your thoughts about this chapter. What stuck out to you from the stories? How can you implement what you read into your life? When you are finished journaling, take some time to pray.

Prayer need: _____
Prayer need: _____
Prayer need: _____

Journal

Chapter Eight
Selfish Christians

"My heart broke for the guys on the street, and my anger raged against all those Christian men."

If anyone has material possessions and sees his brother in need but has no pity on him, how can the love of God be in him?

—1 John 3:17

John

One summer I was attending a Promise Keepers conference with a bunch of men from my church. Promise Keepers puts on huge men's conferences all across America. The one I was attending was in downtown St. Louis at the Savvis Center, and they were expecting over fifteen thousand people. A bunch of us were hanging out in front of the Savvis Center, waiting to go in, when I got the craving for a Diet Coke (I'm addicted, I'll admit it!). I looked into the window of the Savvis Center and noticed it was a Pepsi facility, so I decided to go for a walk to find a Diet Coke before I went in. A friend of mine named Joey went with me. We hadn't made it very far down the road when we ran across four homeless men.

There was one guy, John, who was standing on the street, asking people for money, and three other guys who were sitting on some steps, drinking and sleeping the evening away. Joey and I stopped and started talking to the guys who were on the steps. We introduced ourselves and then started to listen to them as they told us their stories. As we continued to talk, they started asking us questions because they found out we were pastors. Then they started asking us to pray for them. I prayed with one guy because he was missing his fingers. It wasn't like they had gotten cut off or he was born without them because you could see where the bones came out of his skin by his knuckles. It looked as if his fingers had fallen off. Another guy asked Joey to pray for him. Joey wrapped his arm around the man and started praying. For the rest of the time we were there, the man wouldn't leave Joey's side. He had finally found someone who loved him.

We were having a great time ministering to these guys, but John wasn't so happy. Remember John? He was the one who was working the street. Every couple of minutes he'd yell at the other homeless men, "Hey, get up here and help me get some money!" But the other guys wouldn't move. He was yelling pretty loud and getting pretty angry, but the other guys just sat there. He was starting to get so irritated that it was concerning me, and it should have.

The next thing I knew he had walked up behind me and pulled out his knife. He drew the blade and put it right in front of my face and said, "Hey, see my blade?"

"Yeah, that's a nice one."

Fortunately for me he wasn't in the mood to use it. Instead, he started talking. As he was talking, the other guys filled him in on the details of who we were. It floored him we were pastors. From that point on he never referred to me again as Josh, but instead as "Cool Cat Pastor."

We ended up having a great time talking to John. It became pretty obvious he was the ringleader of the crew. He had been living on the streets for several years. He shared with us stories of his wife and daughter. I asked him when was the last time he had talked to them, and he told me it was years ago. Joey reached out his phone and said, "Call them." So John picked up the phone and called his daughter. It was awesome to see this drunk, cursing, knife-wielding homeless man talking to his daughter with tears in his eyes. It had been a good night of ministry.

We got up to take off, but before we left I wanted to ask John one more question. I said, "Do you know what is going on in the Savvis Center tonight?"

He said, "Yeah, I know it's some type of Christian event for men."

I replied, "Yeah, there are about fifteen thousand men walking down this street tonight to go to this event. So tell me, how did you do? Were you able to make some decent money tonight?"

His reply cut me to the heart and made my blood boil. He said, "This is the worst night ever. We haven't gotten jack squat and, to be honest, you guys are the first guys of the entire night to even acknowledge us."

My heart broke for the guys on the street, and my anger raged against all those Christian men.

Selfish or Selfless

Are you selfish or selfless? How many times have you been just like those men, so concerned about getting to church or worship so you could spend time with God? So concerned about being there yourself you forgot about taking others to be with him? That was the whole problem on the street that night. Fifteen thousand men wanted to get to Promise Keepers so they could be with God. Fifteen thousand men were more concerned about their own spiritual health than the spiritual health of others. Does that happen to you? Do you find yourself not inviting people to church because church is for you? Do you find yourself upset when you see someone's needs at church because you know they are possibly going to take some of your precious time?

Evangelism takes time and it takes sacrifice. Think about the feeding of the five thousand recorded in Matthew 14:15. Jesus had just heard about John the Baptist's death. Upon hearing this, he hopped in a boat and withdrew to a solitary place to be alone, but when

Selfish Christians

he landed on the seashore he saw thousands of people, and his heart broke for them. He had compassion on the people and healed all the sick who were there. He ended up spending the entire day with them, loving them, healing them, and preaching to them.

As evening approached, the disciples made one of the most idiotic statements in the entire Bible. They said, "Send them away." The disciples were getting hungry, so they wanted Jesus to send the people away. The people there were hearing the words of God, the words of life! They were getting everything they needed, but the disciples were so concerned about their own hunger that they wanted Jesus to stop feeding the crowd.

Unfortunately, I know many Christians who do the very same thing. They are so concerned about getting to church they forget about helping someone else get there. People are too wrapped up in their own lives to stop and help the life of another.

Jesus always had time for those in need. In Luke 7, Jesus noticed a funeral going down the street. A widow was leading a funeral procession for her son. Luke 7:13 says, "When the Lord saw her, his heart went out to her and he said, 'Don't cry.'"

Think about the words in that verse. He saw her and his heart went out to her. But it didn't stop with just noticing her or feeling sorry for her. He then went up and touched the coffin and raised the young man from the dead. He took time to stop.

He did it again in Matthew 20:29–34. Two blind men heard Jesus was coming and started crying out, "Lord, Son of David, have mercy on us." Immediately, the crowd told the two guys to quiet down. The crowd didn't think the blind men were worth Jesus' time, but he did. He heard their cry for mercy and stopped and healed them.

Think about the Good Samaritan's story in Luke 10. There was a man who got beaten up and was lying on the road bleeding. A priest walked right by him and ignored him because the priest was busy. A Levite, who is a religious man, walked past him because he didn't want to get dirty. But the Samaritan picked up the man and cared for his needs.

These stories teach us that no matter how tired or busy we are, we must stop. People are always worth it. It takes time and sacrifice to share your faith and minister to people. When you are given an opportunity, will you stop?

Questions to Ponder

What did you learn from John's story?

When was the last time you passed someone who needed help? Did you help him? Why or why not?

What can you learn from the story of the feeding of the five thousand? Do you see times in your church or youth group when you "send them away"?

Pray God will put someone in your path to whom you can be a Good Samaritan.

Scriptures to Study

> Luke 10:25–37
> Matthew 9:10–13
> Hebrews 13:2

Selfish Christians

Thoughts and Prayers

Spend some time journaling your thoughts about this chapter. What stuck out to you from the stories? How can you implement what you read into your life? When you are finished journaling, take some time to pray.

Prayer need: _____
Prayer need: _____
Prayer need: _____

Journal

_____

_____

Chapter Nine
Eyes of Innocence

"When you look into people's eyes, you can see their soul."

The eye is the lamp of the body.

—Matt. 6:22

Tracy

One day I was walking through the Fremont Experience in Las Vegas. The Fremont Experience is a street in downtown Vegas that has been restored. The famous old casino, The Horseshoe, is located on it. The famous neon cowgirl and cowboy signs hang on the side of a couple of buildings. And a historic strip club, called the Glitter Gulch, is located right in the middle of it all.

It was in front of the Glitter Gulch that I saw Tracy. She was dressed in a skimpy, metallic outfit and wore a bleached blonde wig. She was standing in front of the strip club, trying to get guys' attention. She would try to get a guy to come over and talk to her with the hope of taking him inside to dance for him. I felt God telling me to go talk to her, so I walked toward her.

As I got closer, my heart started to break, especially when I saw her eyes. Her eyes were the young eyes of innocence. When I looked into them, I couldn't believe how young she looked. She barely could have been over the age of eighteen. Behind the outfit, the fake hair, and all the makeup, there was raw innocence, innocence in the idea that she was just a young girl who had made a wrong turn in life. I could see a young girl who had gotten herself into a lifestyle of sin and a life on the street. My heart broke for this young daughter of God.

I stood around and talked to Tracy for a while. We talked about life, Vegas, and her story. As we talked, I realized she wasn't just a stripper, she was also a prostitute. She used her body to make a living. The more she talked and the more I heard how this beautiful young girl was destroying her life, the more my heart broke.

At one point while we were talking, I asked how she felt about God. She said she believed in him and loved him, but knew she wasn't living for him. I asked if she had ever thought about attending a church. With that she kind of stepped back and said, "Yeah, right, like I would be accepted there." She continued by saying, "You know that I strip for people and sell my body. The church is the last place I would want to go."

Eyes of Innocence

I wanted to try to convince her, but I knew she was right. I knew many churches would look at her with judgmental eyes. They would see her sin and not her young eyes of innocence. We talked for a little longer and I assured her I loved her and God loves her, and then I walked away.

Usually when I have encounters with people on the street, I leave the encounter with a burden for the person I talked to, but also with a joy, knowing I was able to encourage and love them. But it was different when I walked away from Tracy. When I walked away from her I felt burdened, but I had no joy. I was ticked off that I didn't know of a church that would accept her. When I got home I wrote her a long letter and enclosed in the envelope a sermon I had preached about how God loves you no matter what. I mailed it to the "Glitter Gulch" with her name on it, hoping it would get to her. I will never know if it did or not, but it was my attempt to help a young girl feel accepted.

Eyes of Innocence

I keep referring to Tracy's eyes because I believe you can tell so much about people through their eyes. When I looked at everything in Tracy's life, I could see sin, sin, sin. But as I looked into her eyes, I saw a young girl dying to live, a young girl who was trapped inside a body of sin. Matthew 6:22 says, "The eye is the lamp of the body." When you look into someone's eyes, you can see that person's soul. Don't look at a person's lifestyle. Don't look at their sins. Don't look at all the bad things they are doing. Look into their eyes, deep into their eyes, and see the soul inside that God loves.

I looked into the eyes of Tracy, the stripper and prostitute, just like Jesus looked into the eyes of a prostitute in Luke 7:36–50. A man named Simon invited Jesus to come to his house for dinner. When Jesus showed up at Simon's house, Simon invited him in but didn't wash his feet, kiss his cheek, or anoint him with oil, which, according to tradition, he should have done.

While they were sitting at the table, the town prostitute snuck into the room. She walked over to where Jesus was and knelt down at his feet. She then started weeping, kissing Jesus' feet and anointing them with oil.

Simon was angry with the woman and perplexed by Jesus because he wasn't stopping her. Eventually, Jesus looked straight down at the woman, while saying to Simon, "Do you see this woman? I came into your house. You did not give me any water for my feet, but she wet my feet with her tears and wiped them with her hair. You did not give me a kiss, but this woman, from the time I entered, has not stopped kissing my feet. You did not put oil on my head, but she has poured perfume on my feet" (Luke 7:44–46).

I believe the coolest part of this story is not what Jesus said but what he did. He looked the woman in the eye. He showed this woman he loved her and accepted her praise by looking deep into her eyes. I bet when Jesus looked into her eyes he didn't see a dirty prostitute. Instead, he saw the innocent, childish eyes of a daughter. No one else would love this sinful woman. No one else would accept her. She was just like Tracy. If she had gone to the town church (the synagogue), she would have been

Eyes of Innocence

judged and stared at, just like Tracy and just like many people you encounter in your school, workplace, and community. It is time for us to open our doors, because there are Tracys everywhere.

Tracy #2

One weekend I was preaching at my church. I was challenging our church to become a place where people could find healing, love, and Jesus. I said we need to be known as a place where lost people will be accepted. To illustrate this point, I told them Tracy's story. I told them she was a stripper and a prostitute in Vegas. I told them she said a church is the last place she would want to be because she knew she would be judged and not accepted.

When I finished telling her story, I said, "We have got to be a place where Tracys are welcomed."

Right after that I offered an invitation and told people if they needed to come forward to accept Christ as their Savior, to do so. Or if they needed to come forward to repent of their judgmental attitudes toward lost people, then to do so.

As the band was playing, a young lady walked up to me and said, "I'm Tracy!"

At first I was a little confused, and then she said it again: "I'm Tracy!" Well, I knew she wasn't Tracy from Vegas; she didn't look anything like her, but what she told me next made me understand why she was Tracy.

She told me her name was Tracy and she was a stripper and prostitute. She said she'd wanted to come to church for a long time, but she was afraid no one would accept her. That morning she'd gotten up enough courage to attend church. As I was telling my story, she was hearing her story.

She then said she wanted to repent and accept Jesus as her Savior. I stood there with my head spinning. I just couldn't get over the providence of God. I felt like I hadn't done much to help Tracy from Vegas to come to Jesus, but because of my encounter with her I was able to help Tracy from Illinois to come to Jesus.

What happened next was just another thing straight from God. When I got done praying with Tracy and telling her more about Jesus she said, "I need to tell the church that I'm a stripper and a prostitute."

I replied, "Tracy, you don't need to tell them that. We'll just tell them you just accepted Jesus, but we don't have to tell them you are a prostitute."

But she wouldn't accept that as an answer. She insisted on telling them, so I said, "OK."

After the invitation, I introduced Tracy and said she had some things she wanted to say. She then took the microphone and confessed to them that she was a prostitute and asked for help. Immediately, women from all over the church got up out of their seats and came up to Tracy and started hugging her, praying for her, and crying with her. The church was being "the church," and I just had to step back. That day I saw a church look into the eyes of a woman and see the innocence of a child.

Questions to Ponder

What did you learn from the story of Tracy from Vegas?

Why is it important to spiritually look into someone's eyes? Do you more often look at the outside and see the sin or the inside and see the soul?

Tracy from Vegas said, "Why would I want to go to church and be judged? I won't be accepted." What would you have said in response to her?

What did you learn from the story of Tracy from Illinois?

In your opinion, how would your church or youth group have responded to either Tracy?

Commit to, the next time you hear someone confess he or she is having a hard time with a sin, going to that person and accepting, loving, and helping him or her.

Scriptures to Study

James 2:1–6
Mark 10:13–16
Mark 9:42
Matthew 4:23–25

Thoughts and Prayers

Spend some time journaling your thoughts about this chapter. What stuck out to you from the stories? How can you implement what you read into your life? When you are done journaling, spend some time praying.

Prayer need: _____
Prayer need: _____
Prayer need: _____

Journal

_____

_____

Chapter Ten

Give Up

"What breaks your heart should move your hands."

And everyone who has left houses or brothers or sisters or father or mother or children or fields for my sake will receive a hundred times as much and will inherit eternal life.

—Matt. 19:29

The Joke's on Me

I received an e-mail that said, "We see that you are coming to Haiti. Don't leave Haiti without taking one of our beautiful orphans home with you." I read the e-mail and then sent it on to my wife as a joke. She called me later that day and said, "Clay, Mackenzie, (my two older children), and I have talked about it, and we want to do it!" My jaw hit the ground and I let her know I was just joking. We talked for a little while and left the conversation by saying we'd talk about it at dinner.

That night as we sat around the dinner table, we talked about whether or not we should adopt a child from Haiti. We read the story of a little boy named Tate who needed a home. Tate was born into poverty. His mom was fourteen years old when she delivered him. She tried to care for him but was unable to and abandoned him.

A missionary was walking through the village when she saw Tate lying on the side of the road. She quickly made her way toward him to care for him. When she picked him up, his body was totally stiff from dehydration. She took him back to her medical mission and nursed him back to health. He was eleven months old and weighed a mere eleven pounds.

The missionary found the mom and asked if she wanted her boy back and if she could care for him. The young mom said yes and took Tate back. Unfortunately, a couple of weeks later the missionary found Tate on the side of the road in bad condition again. She took him in and nursed him back to health, but this time the mom didn't want anything to do with him.

My family was jumping to adopt Tate, but I was pulling back the reins. I quickly let my kids know that, yeah, we need to help take care of the poor and orphans, but to adopt him would cost a ton of money. I told them we didn't have that type of money.

Immediately, Clay, who was eight at the time, said, "I'll sell my dirt bike!" He had received a Honda XR 80 for his birthday three months earlier.

Mackenzie, who was six, said, "I'll give up my dance classes!"

I was so proud of their willingness to sacrifice, but I knew even that would just make a small dent in the overall cost. I knew adopting Tate would cost us all of our assets and require us to take a second mortgage on our house. I tabled the discussion with the comment, "Let's pray about it for a while." But what I really was saying was, let's give it time, and hopefully you will forget about it.

A few weeks passed and there were occasional talks about Tate, but it came to a head one night while I was preaching. I had to speak at an event in Des Moines. That night I was preaching from Luke 7, and I was talking about things that break your heart: the poor, the lost, those who are hurting. From there I moved to my last point and said, "What breaks your heart should move your hands." As soon as I said that, it was as if I heard God speak directly to me as he said, "Shut up and get off the stage or do what I'm calling you to do." I knew at that moment that God wanted me to use my hands to take care of Tate. When I finished preaching that night, I first went to a corner and wept before the Lord, and then I called my wife and told her to start the paperwork.

That's only the first part of the story. The second part came in the form of a little girl named Abbey. Right before we turned in our paperwork, we got another e-mail from the orphanage. They informed us they had a little girl for whom they couldn't find a home. She was also the child of a fourteen-year-old mom. The mom was homeless and did her best to care for the baby, but it was just becoming impossible. She knew her daughter would be better off if she gave her up for adoption, so that is what she did.

Abbey came to the orphanage at the same time as Tate, so they were used to being together. There were only eight days separating them in age, so the orphanage wanted to know if we would like to have "twins." Again, my heart wanted to, but I just couldn't see any financial way to do it. We had tapped out every aspect of our finances. When I looked at the cost, I knew we were $3,000 short, and the only way we could come up with that was if God placed it in our lap.

After praying some more and seeking counsel from a friend, my wife and I decided to add Abbey to our family as well and put our faith in God that he would provide the $3,000 that we were short. And he did.

On July 2, 2003, my wife and I went to Haiti to pick up our children. Two days later we boarded a plane back to America with them. Tate and Abbey Finklea became United States citizens on July 4, 2003. I have a wife and four children who make up my family. Oh, it cost…but it is worth it

Give Up Everything

If you want to be a disciple and share your faith, it will cost you. The adoption cost me, but it was well worth it. Because of the adoption, my kids learned about sacrifice, we followed the Scripture's commands to take care of the poor and orphans, and I get to share the gospel with my children and teach them the ways of God. Tate and Abbey probably would have died at young ages and, if they had lived, they would have lived in poverty and probably would not have heard about Jesus Christ. Because they are part of my family, they now hang out at church all the time and hear the message of Christ daily.

I learned a valuable lesson through the adoption process because it cost me dearly. To be a disciple and to share your faith, you have to be willing to give up everything. Is that a price you are willing to pay?

Luke 14:25–35 talks about the cost of discipleship. It breaks the cost into three areas. The first thing Jesus says it will cost you to follow him is your loved ones. Luke 14:26 says, "If anyone comes to me and does not hate his father and mother, his wife and children, his brothers and sisters he cannot be my disciple." If you truly want to be a disciple of Christ and you want to share your faith, then you must realize God must come before your loved ones. Many times we put our loved ones above God, especially our friends. I've seen tons of high school students who don't allow God anywhere near their friends. It is as if we don't want to hurt our friendships because of our belief in God. I know a lot of students who tell me they want to share Christ with their friends but don't want to upset them or ruin their friendship.

My question to you is this: Do you love your friend or the friendship more? If you love the friends over the friendships, then you will do whatever it takes to tell them about God, even if it ruins a friendship. If you love a friendship more than a friend, then you won't bring up God because you are afraid you might ruin the friendship even though your disobedience might lead your friend to an eternal punishment in hell. Do you get it? Love God more than your friends and loved ones. If you love God more, then you won't be ashamed to share him with your loved ones.

The second cost that is talked about in Luke 14 is your life. If you want to be a disciple and share your faith, it will cost you your life. Verse 27 says, "And anyone who does not carry his cross and follow me cannot be my disciple." You must be willing to sacrifice your life if you want to follow him. You must be willing to put the cross on your shoulder and carry it everywhere—into the classroom, onto the court, into the mall, and onto the jobsite. This means you must be willing to put your own dreams to the side and follow God's dreams. You must be willing to trade in your "American Jesus" for a "World Jesus."

An American Jesus philosophy is one that says, "I need to go to a great college and get a good degree so I can get a high-paying salary to buy a large house where I can raise my wife and kids and send them off to a great college. And as long as I go to church on weekends and put a little bit of money in the offering plate, then I'm doing exactly what my American Jesus would want me to do." You have the American Jesus and the American dream.

A World Jesus philosophy is one that says, "I am willing to surrender every aspect of my career, family, finances, dreams, and future for the growth of the kingdom of God." If you subscribe to an American Jesus, when you die you will look back over your life and see your footprints in the dirt. But if you adopt the attitude of a World Jesus, when you die and look back at the dirt all you will see is a skid mark of a cross being dragged behind you.

Third, you must be willing to give up your little things. Verse 33 says, "In the same way, any of you who does not give up everything he has cannot be my disciple." That seems like an impossible verse. You must be willing to give up everything you own, everything you have, everything you desire, and every little thing attached to you. When you give up every little thing you have, then God can use you because there is nothing for you to worry about. You realize you own nothing, but God owns everything. When this becomes your reality, you will be following him and helping others to do the same. You not only will be in step with the Lord, but your sacrifice will help many others to be in step with him also. Yeah, it costs to be a disciple and to lead others to him, but it is worth it!

Faith In Action

I want to challenge you to put this verse into action right now. I work with an organization called Compassion International. Compassion joins with churches all over the world in the fight against poverty. You can partner with them by sponsoring a child. For a little more than a dollar a day, you can give a kid food, clothing, shelter, and Jesus. Last year over eighty thousand kids accepted Christ because of people who were willing to do what it cost. Will you? Please go to www.compassion.com and sign up to sponsor a child. It will cost, but it is worth it.

QUESTIONS TO PONDER

What did you learn from the adoption story?

Has your faith cost you any friendships? Is that good or bad?

Do you have the attitude of an American Jesus or a World Jesus? When you die, do you think people will see your footprints or the cross you dragged?

What little things have you given up? What is the one thing you have been unwilling to give up? Is it time to give it up?

Scriptures to Study

Mark 10:17–22
Luke 5:1–11
Luke 9:57–62

Thoughts and Prayers

Spend some time journaling your thoughts about this chapter. What stuck out to you from the stories? How can you implement what you read into your life? After you are done journaling, spend some time praying.

Prayer need: _____
Prayer need: _____
Prayer need: _____

Journal

Chapter Eleven
Don't Judge the Book

"We are never to judge those outside of the church."

What business is it of mine to judge those outside the church? Are you not to judge those inside? God will judge those outside.
—1 Cor. 5:12

Kris's Phone Call

It was a normal Sunday afternoon, the one day of the week that bored me to death. Since I did not grow up attending church, Sunday was always a dull day. There was never anything to do, and all the TV shows were uninteresting. I recall this particular Sunday being especially boring because it was a cold, nasty winter day.

That's when the phone rang. It was a friend of mine named Kris. We chitchatted for a little while, and then she asked me if I wanted to go to her youth group. She explained to me it was a gathering of students at her church. At first I was a little hesitant, but then I remembered how bored I was, so I said yes.

I met Kris at her church and we went in for youth group. I don't remember the lesson that night, but I do remember having a blast. I actually enjoyed it, which was a shock for me because I thought everything that dealt with church had to be extremely boring. I was pleasantly surprised.

The next week rolled around, and I lived my life as usual until Sunday. On Sunday I caught myself hoping the phone would ring. I sat next to it, waiting for a call from Kris. Sure enough, the phone rang and it was Kris. She invited me to youth group again and I said, "Yeah, I would love to go. I had a great time last week."

This time, I not only had fun, I also learned some things about Christ and his love. I vividly remember the lesson like it was yesterday. The teacher passed out pictures/artwork of Jesus. Each picture was different: Jesus praying over a rock in Gethsemane, Jesus carrying a lamb, Jesus working in a carpenter shop, Jesus with a glow around him, and Jesus with a crown of thorns on his head. The lesson was about the Jesus you identify with the most. When the teacher talked about Jesus and the crown of thorns, my heart started to break. I went home that night and began to think about Jesus a little more.

Don't Judge the Book

Monday hit and I went on with my normal life: school, weights for baseball, homework, hanging with friends, and alcohol. On Friday night a couple of friends and I went skiing all night. For me, it was a little skiing and a lot of drinking.

All day Saturday I felt like crap, and then came Sunday. When I woke up on Sunday my first thought was, *Tonight I get to go to church*. I couldn't believe I was actually excited and looking forward to attending church. My heart had been sparked for God, and I couldn't wait for six o'clock to come around so I could hear more about him. I especially wanted to go on this night because of my Friday night drinking and Saturday hangover. I knew I needed church.

I sat by the phone all afternoon, waiting for it to ring. I was waiting for Kris to call. Finally, I couldn't take it any longer so I called her, but she wasn't home. I wanted to go so bad but didn't know if I could just show up by myself, so I stayed home.

The next day at school I ran into Kris in the hall. I asked her, "Why didn't you call me last night? I really wanted to go to youth group, but I didn't know if I could just show up."

She shot a glare back at me and said, "Why would you want to do that? I heard about Friday night. I heard you went skiing and got wasted. It is obvious by your actions that you don't want to have anything to do with God!"

And at that she turned and walked away.

Judging

Kris missed a possible salvation moment with me. I believe if I had continued to be invited to youth group with Kris, I would have given my life to Christ a lot earlier than I actually did. I was searching at that point in my life. I was living every day for the party, and it was leaving me empty. Sure, I was having fun on Friday, but I was regretting it on Saturday. I had heard the message of the cross the week before, and I was ready to hear more about it.

Unfortunately, Kris was more concerned about my sin than she was my soul. When she said those words to me in the hallway, she turned her God away from me. I know now God hadn't turned away from me, but at that point in my life everything I knew about God was through Kris. Therefore, in my mind, when Kris turned away from me, so did God. That led me deeper into sin than I had ever been.

You must realize when dealing with non-Christians that you can't judge them for their sins. As Christians we can judge Christians, but we cannot judge non-Christians. First Corinthians 5:12 says, "What business is it of mine to judge those outside the church? Are you not to judge those inside? God will judge those outside."

This verse tells us whom we are to judge and whom we are not to judge. First, understand that as Christians we are called to judge those who are inside the church, those who have put their faith in Christ. It is our responsibility to the individual Christian and also to the church to do this. If a friend of yours is a Christian but is living his life in sin, then you must confront him for his sake and also for the sake of the church. First Corinthians 5:1–12 tells us we need to confront brothers who are sinning. By confronting the individual who is in sin, you might lead him to repentance. If he doesn't repent, then he needs to be confronted for the overall health of the church.

The tricky part is figuring out how to do this. Chances are you have a friend who has accepted Christ and goes to church but is living in sin. Try walking up to a friend in church and judging him; you probably will not be well received. Judge, but judge carefully.

First, check yourself out: do you struggle with the same sin your friend does? Have you repented of your own sin problem? Scripture teaches us to get the log out of our eye before we remove the speck of dust from someone else's eye (Luke 6:41).

Second, check your motives. Are you judging someone for the right reason or because you want to confront him?

Third, be sure you have a good relationship with the person before you judge him. If you haven't developed the relationship, then you won't have the ability to help him come to repentance.

Last, speak in love from your heart. Approach the person with an overwhelming amount of love pouring out on him. Let him know you are only talking to him because you absolutely love him and know God has a better plan for his life.

It is our job to judge those who believe and are in the church as a way to hold them accountable. We are never to judge those outside of the church. That's not our job, it's God's. We don't know their hearts. We don't know where they are in the salvation process.

I know if people had looked at me my junior year of high school they would have never seen someone who was searching for God. They would have seen a rebellious, pierced, partying teenager who had an awesome mullet. But even though the outside of me was living for the party, the inside of me was searching for God.

One of the most common excuses you will hear people give for not wanting to go to church is they don't want to be judged. Non-Christians believe people inside of the church will automatically judge them because of their lifestyles, their pasts, their dress, etc. Unfortunately, many times they are right. We Christians have to become people who do not see the sin but rather see the soul.

You can't judge a non-Christian by his appearance or his actions. At any moment he could be one invitation away from accepting Christ. So don't judge your non-Christian friends who are sinning. Love them and continue to be ready to offer them the invitation.

QUESTIONS TO PONDER

What did you learn from the story of Kris and the phone call?

What non-Christians have you been judging because of their actions?

How have your actions been turning your God away from them?

Don't Judge the Book

Who is that one person in your life or school about whom you would say, "There is no way he would ever accept Christ?" What can you do to reach out to him or her?

Scriptures to Study

Psalm 9:7–8
Matthew 7:1–5
John 12:47–48
James 4:11–12

Thoughts and Prayers

Spend some time journaling your thoughts about this chapter. What stuck out to you from the stories? How can you implement what you read into your life? Take some time to pray.

Prayer need: _____
Prayer need: _____
Prayer need: _____

Journal

_____

_____

Chapter Twelve
I Love to Flirt

"Why do we treat evangelism like a hunt?"

Jesus replied, "I will also ask you one question."
—Matt. 21:23

Ally

Sharing your faith is like flirting. As I tell you about my encounters with Ally, you will see my point.

Ally was a girl I met here in Quincy. One night a friend and I went into a bar to get a bite to eat. While we were there, we kept our eyes open and looked up for opportunities to share our faith.

At one point two girls walked by. When one of them glanced over at me, I simply said, "Hello." With that she stopped and started to talk. She was no different from most of the people in the bar that night. She was drunk and looking for people to hang out with.

She and her friend sat down at our booth. She told us her name was Ally, and we started to talk. As we began to talk and laugh, she asked what we did for a living. When we told her we were both ministers, her jaw hit the table (a reaction I'm accustomed to).

"No way," she said. "A church that would allow you guys to be ministers is possibly a church that would allow me to attend." After a little bit of a conversation she and her friend said goodbye and moved to another table.

The next week my friend and I went to the same bar, on that same night, to get something to eat again, and guess whom we saw? Ally was there, and when she saw us she came over and had a seat. We talked some more.

Understand this: when I say we talked, it means we talked about whatever she wanted to talk about. Generally speaking, it was just about life, but every now and then I dropped in a little statement about God or church.

These encounters ended up going on for weeks. Every Wednesday night I would see Ally at a bar, and she would come over and talk. Every week she would ask just a little bit more about God. I answered her questions and gave her my thoughts, but I didn't try to persuade her.

Ally often commented about how important having a god in your life is. She would say things like, "I've tried about every kind of faith out there and I believe they are all good." She believed whether you were Christian,

I Love to Flirt

Buddhist, Wiccan, a Spiritualist, etc., it didn't matter. She said, "All roads lead to the same place."

I knew on the inside she was dead wrong. I knew I could tell her, "Jesus is the way, the truth, and the life and no one gets to the Father except through him." But at that point she didn't need to hear that. All it would have done is push her away.

Instead, I responded to her questions with statements like, "A lot of people think that." I wouldn't necessarily agree with her, but I wouldn't debate her either. My friend questioned why I didn't correct her, and I simply replied it wasn't time yet.

This went on for weeks. Another Wednesday night and another encounter with Ally—until finally one night it was time. As we were sitting at the table talking, a tear welled up in her eye and she asked if we could talk alone (at that time there were five or six other people at the table).

I said, "Sure," and we went to the next table over (that was as far away and as alone as I was willing to be).

When we sat down at the table, she started to weep and share how desperately she had been searching for God and how badly she needed forgiveness. She commented on how empty she felt inside and on her lack of purpose in life. I knew this was the time to move in with the truth. So around that table I started to share with Ally how there was a hole in her heart that was specifically carved out for God, that he is the ONLY way to find forgiveness, life, and purpose. I explained to her all she needed to do was accept him as the true way. The next Sunday, she was at church with me!

Are You a Flirt?

I flirted with Ally—no, not in a traditional way, but in an evangelistic/spiritual way. Normally when people flirt, it means they "make eyes" at others. They keep it on a surface level. They're playful and joyful. True flirts will try to get others to smile at them, share a moment, raise their attention, and then move on. Think about it. If you saw someone who caught your eye and made you think he or she was a possible prospect, would you just walk up and lay a big kiss on that person? Or, instead, would you first make eyes at him or her, flash a smile, and maybe try to get into a quick conversation? You would flirt, not move in for the kill.

Why do we treat evangelism like a hunt? We move in for the kill. Many people try to evangelize someone by basically laying a big kiss on him or her right at the beginning rather than just flirting.

People meet someone and ask:

"Do you know Jesus as your Savior?"

"Have you been saved?"

"If you die today, do you know where you are going to spend eternity?"

I'm not saying statements like those never work, but generally speaking that's not the ideal way to evangelize. The best way is to take your time and first establish a relationship with an unsaved person by "spiritually" flirting.

I Love to Flirt

Think about Jesus and his two encounters recorded in John 3 and 4. Throughout both encounters, he flirted. In John 3, a prominent man named Nicodemus came to Jesus and started asking him questions. Did you notice that Jesus didn't immediately answer his questions? Instead, he "flirted" back with more questions and short statements. Jesus could have confronted Nicodemus right then, but instead he gave him time to think through things. He offered him time to go back and truly consider these new thoughts about God. This allowed him to accept them in his own time. Jesus flirted with Nicodemus.

In the same manner, he flirted with the woman at the well in John 4. The woman at the well was totally opposite of Nicodemus. Nicodemus was a man of stature, but the woman at the well was a woman of shame. He treated both individuals the same. He flirted with them. The woman came toward the well, and he asked her a simple question: "Will you get me a drink?" From a simple question came a long conversation where Jesus didn't confront or condemn the woman. He simply engaged in a conversation with her and let it take its natural course.

What is interesting about these two conversations is one brought an immediate harvest and one produced a harvest later. The woman at the well immediately recognized Jesus as Lord, but Nicodemus didn't, to our knowledge, until later. It doesn't matter that one was immediate and one was later. What matters is that in both instances Jesus flirted and by doing so brought in a harvest.

Author Brian McLaren describes this as dancing. He says you move in and dance with someone for a while. When the song's over you don't ask "who won," but rather you look forward to another dance. The point is this: Don't try to debate with someone about Jesus. Don't try to answer every question immediately or defend every aspect of your faith. Remember, Ally was saying things in the beginning that were very contrary to my faith, but instead of debating with her I slid over them, knowing if I stayed committed to the relationship I would have an opportunity to give her my Jesus.

Questions to Ponder

What did you learn from Ally's story?

Explain in your own words how you can evangelistically flirt with someone.

Do you try to "win" every time you talk to someone about Jesus? How can you do a better job of "flirting" with your friends?

Scriptures to Study

John 3:1–12
John 4:4–26
Jude 22–23
1 Thessalonians 4:11–12
Colossians 4:6

Thoughts and Prayers

Spend some time journaling your thoughts about this chapter. What stuck out to you from the stories?

I Love to Flirt

How you can implement what you read into your life? When you are finished journaling, take some time to pray.

Prayer need: _____
Prayer need: _____
Prayer need: _____

Journal

_____

_____

Chapter Thirteen
Rock Bottom

"The best time to tell someone about Jesus is when his heart is broken."

The sacrifices of God are a broken spirit; a broken and contrite heart.
—Ps. 51:17

My Story: Hitting Rock Bottom

My story is about how God took a dirty, rotten, sinful boy and turned him into a man who could be used by him.

Even before I was born, my mom and dad were having marital problems, but when I arrived and the doctors told my dad I had birth defects, it put him over the top and he split. To this day I've never seen my real dad.

I was born with birth defects in my head. I was born with two eardrums in each ear, which caused me to be deaf. I also had birth defects that caused my sinus passages to be blocked. The combination of these two things caused pressure to build up in my head to the point doctors were afraid my head would "pop." They told my mom they were going to have to do surgery on me, and the chances of survival were slim. They were afraid that when they slit my eardrums, causing the pressure to be released, that it could lead to immediate death. They said if I survived there was a great chance I would have brain damage or be mentally retarded. In addition to that, the doctors said there was no chance of my hearing ever being restored.

The first surgery took place when I was five weeks old. The surgery was successful, but it was just the beginning of more to come. Over the next eighteen months, I had four more surgeries. And to everyone's surprise, I was totally fine—even to the point that when I was almost two years old my hearing was restored.

Unfortunately, though, rather than using my hearing to listen to God I used it to listen to the world. At a young age I started walking down the wrong path. When I was in second grade, I experimented with alcohol and marijuana for the first time, and unfortunately it wasn't my last. From that point on I started walking further and further down the wrong path. My junior-high years were spent trying to be cool and find myself. My high school years were filled with parties, drugs, alcohol, and girls. I did things that were so awful that even as I write this I am brought to tears because of my past. My only purpose was to live for the next sin. I had no direction in life. I didn't care about school or getting an education. All I cared about was having fun and enjoying life.

I finally hit rock bottom at the beginning of my senior year in high school. My sins started catching up with me one after another. It was as if I were in quicksand. The more I tried to get out, the more I sank. I finally hit rock bottom one night when a friend approached me and asked if I would help him do something. And in the process of doing it, we committed a felony offense.

When I got home that night, I went straight to my bedroom, fell onto my bed, and started to cry. I cried like I had never cried before. As I was on my bed weeping, I started reflecting on my life. My life sickened me. There was nothing I could reflect on in my life that was worth remembering. Everything about it made me sick.

With that in my head, I started praying. Now, understand something—I knew nothing about God. No one in my family was a Christian. No one I hung out with worshiped God or attended church. I had been to church only a couple of times in my entire life. I knew nothing about prayer or God, but I remember exactly what I said to God that night. As I lay there weeping, I said, "God, I don't know if you exist. God, I don't know how to pray. God, I don't know if you can hear me, but if you can, help me." My heart was broken and I knew I needed a life change.

Broken Heart Moments

A broken heart is what you need to be looking for because it is in "broken heart times" that people come to Christ. You can ask any Christian who didn't grow up in a church when he gave his life to Christ and most will say it was at a point in his life when his heart was broken. Even in your own spiritual growth, chances are your faith has grown the most at a time in your life when your heart was broken. God expects that, and he desires it. Psalm 51:17 says a broken heart is an acceptable offering to God.

This is a crucial element in evangelism. The best time to tell people about Jesus is when their hearts are broken. You must constantly be looking for times when your friends and people with whom you come in contact are going through tough times. When your friend is going through a tough time, when his heart is broken, that is when you need to be there for him with the gospel. You must be ready to give him the Word at that exact moment because that is when he is most apt to accept it.

Think about the bleeding woman who is mentioned in Luke 7. Here was a woman who had been bleeding for twelve years. She had a menstrual problem that had been continuous, every day, for twelve straight years. She had done everything she possibly could to find a cure. She had spent everything she had on doctors, but to no avail. She was at the point of giving up when she heard Jesus was passing through town. So as a last ditch effort, she pressed her way through the crowd and touched the edge of his cloak, hoping to find healing. When she touched the edge of his garment, immediately power passed from Jesus to her and she was healed.

Rock Bottom

The woman's heart had been broken due to her illness. She was considered a social outcast. She wasn't allowed to be around her family. She wasn't allowed to even go to the temple to worship God because she was "unclean." Yet it was because her heart was broken that she was ready to try Jesus. It was her broken heart that caused her to fight her way through the crowd to touch Jesus. Not only was she immediately healed, she was immediately recognized by Jesus. He turned and looked for the woman, not because she was in trouble or had done a wrong thing, but because he wanted to find this brokenhearted woman and love her.

You need to keep an eye on your friends. When you see them in desperate times with a broken heart, connect them to Jesus. It is the best time to share Christ with someone. Therefore, be looking for people with broken hearts.

The Rest of My Story: An Answered Prayer

I fell asleep that night weeping and praying. When I awoke the next morning, things were different. I hadn't accepted Jesus that night, but my heart was looking for something different. What is amazing is that over the next couple of weeks God started orchestrating a way for me to hear about him. I met a girl named Michelle, and she invited me to attend her youth group. I attended her youth group and enjoyed it. I then attended her church and experienced God for the first time. Within weeks of praying that prayer on my bed, God moved people into my life who led me to Christ. On November 1, 1987, I accepted Jesus as my Savior. God took my broken heart and put it back together through his grace and love.

Today, I am still amazed God could forgive all of my sins and the evil that was inside of me. Not only has he forgiven me, he now even uses me. He is truly amazing. I know this because one day I hit rock bottom and it was there I met Jesus.

Questions to Ponder

What did you learn from my story?

List a couple of times when you have had a broken heart. How did your faith grow in those times?

The bleeding woman tried many things in life, but it wasn't until she tried Jesus that she was healed. What do you see people trying in life in their attempts to find purpose and fulfillment?

Whom do you know who has a broken heart right now? How can you minister to that person today?

Make a commitment that the next time you see someone with a broken heart you will go and minister to him or her.

Scriptures to Study

Psalm 51
John 11:17–37
Luke 22:54–62
Matthew 11:28–30

Rock Bottom

Thoughts and Prayers

Spend some time journaling your thoughts about this chapter. What stuck out to you from the stories? How you can implement what you read into your life? When finished journaling, spend some time praying.

Prayer need: _____
Prayer need: _____
Prayer need: _____

Journal

_____

_____

Chapter Fourteen
I Hate Religion

"Religion screws people up."

Woe to you, blind guides.

—Matt. 23:16

Joab and Judy

I woke up early one morning while I was visiting a friend in Las Vegas. I had actually gone to Vegas to pray over the city and the lost people, so I was setting out that morning to go pray.

I took my Bible and journal and headed for the water fountains at the Bellagio. (If you haven't seen them, these are fountains that shoot huge blasts of water synchronized to music. They are frequently featured on TV shows about Vegas). I anticipated it would be a great place to go spend some time with God, praying for the city. As I was getting close to the Bellagio, I noticed a McDonald's and went in to get my morning ritual of a McMuffin and a Diet Coke. That's when I met Joab and Judy.

Joab was a designer-jean-wearing punk. Not punk as a brat, but punk as a style. He had done a great job of mixing two styles that don't normally go together: expensive clothes and punk. He had jet-black hair, eyeliner, a ripped-up shirt, $250 Diesel jeans, Chuck Taylor shoes, and a multitude of facial piercings. In addition to his look, he had an attitude. He was extremely loud, obnoxious, and vulgar. On top of that, it was obvious he was stoned out of his mind.

Judy was just as high, but very different in appearance. Her style was shown in her lack of clothes. She got noticed not for what she was wearing but for what she wasn't. Her attitude was much different as well. She didn't talk much. She just giggled, laughed, and stared off into space.

Joab was standing in front of me in line and was being loud and obnoxious, yelling at everyone. At one point he turned to me, but rather than yell at me he just looked at me and started up a conversation. He handed me his card and then invited me to a club that night on the Strip.

After that, he stepped up to one register, and I stepped up to the other. I started to order but had to stop because I couldn't help but hear Joab ordering next to me. He was yelling at the top of his lungs, "I want an Egg McMuffin, but don't put the egg on it. I'm allergic to eggs and if I eat one I'll swell up. So whatever you do, don't put egg on it. I'm telling you if you put egg on it, I'll kill you!"

Then he yelled to the cook, "I'm telling you if you put egg on my sandwich I'll jump across this counter, rip off your head, and puke into your neck!" (He threw a lot of cusswords into his speech, which I am leaving out here.)

You could hear a pin drop in the restaurant at this point. When he was done yelling, he turned to me and asked, "Would you like to eat breakfast with me and my wife?"

I thought, *Oh I live for moments like this*, and simply replied, "Yes."

We went outside to the patio and started talking. Judy was feeding her sandwich to the birds (I think she thought she was a bird, she was so high). Joab, when he wasn't yelling at the people at the tables next to us, was sharing his life story with me.

I was listening to one of the saddest stories I'd ever heard. Joab told me he was a nightclub promoter for a club on the strip. Every Thursday through Sunday, he walked around Vegas in the evening and invited people to his club. He worked at the club until three or so in the morning and then went to an after-hours party to have sex and get high. Those parties would go from three o'clock or so until around six or seven in the morning. That is why he was at McDonald's. He was just coming from a party and was still extremely high. His wife, Judy, was a stripper in one of the Vegas clubs, and together they were making a ton of money. They owned a home in Vegas that they lived in Thursday through Sunday. Monday through Wednesday, they lived in their other home in Los Angeles.

I ended up hanging out with Joab and Judy for six hours. We sat at McDonald's for the longest time and then from there went to a couple of cool clothing stores and some CD shops. Throughout our day together, we talked about a ton of different things: life, music, clothes, Vegas, poetry, and religion.

When we talked about religion, I figured out Joab's and Judy's problems. It wasn't the drugs that had screwed up Joab's life, it was his religious upbringing. He grew up in the Mormon faith and ran away from home at the age of eighteen because of all the rules. Judy grew up a Jehovah's Witness and ran away from home at seventeen, thinking there had to be more to life.

Their religion had ruined them. Joab knew all of the verses. He knew the Bible stories and the ways of faith. But that was it. He knew of a religion, not a relationship. Religion had pushed him away from God and into a life of sin.

A Relationship, Not a Religion

Joab and Judy had two major problems I was combating that day. Their first problem was the lifestyle they were living. The second was religion. Neither is an easy problem to fight.

Their lifestyle is one people outside of Christ dream of. They were both very well known in two major cities in America. They were in the middle of the club/entertainment scene. They had more money, clothes, drugs, and friends than they could want. They were living in utopia in their minds.

There was nothing I could say at this point that would help them realize they needed Christ. They had everything they could possibly want. They didn't need anything else. They had developed an appetite for sin, and it was being fulfilled. Their sinful cravings were being fed and their stomachs were getting full.

Sin is wrong, but for many, sin is fulfilling. I'm sure you have many friends who have developed the same type of appetite Joab and Judy had—maybe not to the same degree, but still an appetite for sin. The best thing you can do is live the life in front of them and plant seeds whenever you can. Eventually their appetites will make them sick. If you have an authentic relationship with them, then maybe you will be able to help them when this happens.

In addition to this, religion is what screwed up Joab and Judy. False teaching about God led them into a life of sin. A life they loved. If I had tried to push God on them at all, they would have slammed the door in my face. Religion, in their minds, was the last thing they needed.

Jesus preached about religion when he confronted the teachers of the law and the Pharisees in Matthew 23. He called them hypocrites, vipers, blind guides, and sons of hell because they were teaching people to be religious but not leading people to a relationship with God. The same problem that existed in Jesus' time exists today. People don't want to have anything to do with God because they don't want to have anything to do with religion. It is our job to promote a relationship to people, not a religion.

Therefore, I knew the very best thing I could do for Joab and Judy was show them a Christian who wasn't a religious, rule-following freak, but rather a man who loved having a relationship with God. I needed to demonstrate through my actions that I loved God and loved them. Unfortunately, I knew my actions that day weren't going to save Joab and Judy, and worse than that I was leaving Vegas the next day, and knew I probably wouldn't ever see Joab again.

What Joab and Judy needed more than anything was a Christian to enter their lives—a Christian who would build up a friendship with them and show them a true relationship. Because one day they will crash. Life is great right now in their eyes, but one day the rug will be pulled out from under them. That is when they will be most open to the idea of Christ. But will there be anyone there to share Christ with them?

The lesson you need to learn from Joab and Judy is twofold. First, look for people who are non-Christians and build up friendships with them so when they hit rock bottom and are looking for God you will be there to share Christ with them. They will listen to a friend before they listen to a stranger.

Second, realize religion screws up people. God doesn't call us to a religion but to a relationship. That relationship starts with you. You must have an intimate, personal relationship with Christ. When people see that true relationship, they will see something they want. When they start asking you questions, make sure you give them the answers on how to have a relationship with Christ. Not a religion, but a relationship.

I don't know if I'll ever help Joab and Judy to find that relationship. But there is one thing I do know: every time I'm in Vegas I go to a certain club and ask if Joab is working.

Questions to Ponder

What did you learn from the story about Joab and Judy?

Whom do you know who loves the life of sin he is living?

Whom do you know who has been screwed up by religion or the church?

List some specific ways you can build relationships with these individuals. How can you best minister to them?

Scriptures to Study

Matthew 23
Matthew 6:5–6
James 1:26–27
Matthew 13:1–9, 19–23

Thoughts and Prayers

Spend some time journaling your thoughts about this chapter. What stuck out to you from the stories? How can you implement what you read into your life? Spend some time praying.

Prayer need: _____
Prayer need: _____
Prayer need: _____

Journal

_____

_____

Chapter Fifteen

Empty

"The only thing that can take care of the emptiness is a relationship with Jesus."

For you know that it was not with perishable things such as silver or gold that you were redeemed from the empty way of life handed down to you by your forefathers, but with the precious blood of Christ.
—1 Peter 1:18–19

Stacey

I met Stacey one night as I was leaving a bar in Quincy. I had been in the bar eating some dinner, and as I was walking out, Stacey literally ran into me. She came around the corner of the hall and ran straight into me. I don't think she saw me because she was totally blitzed. She could barely stand up.

After she ran into me, she looked up at me, stared into my eyes, and slurred, "I know you!"

I just laughed with her and said, "You do?"

She replied, "Yeah, you were in the paper. You're the bar pastor."

(The newspaper had heard that I spend a lot of time in bars and on streets in Quincy trying to minister to people. So they did a story on me about both this and the things we were doing in our church to reach the lost. I really didn't think it was that big of a deal, but it ended up being on the front page of the Sunday paper.)

I smiled and said, "Well, you can call me that or you can just call me Josh."

In her drunken stupor, she just kept laughing and saying, "You're the bar pastor. What are you doing in my bar?"

"Your bar?" I asked. "What makes this your bar?"

She answered, "I work here, but I'm off tonight. Can't you tell?" Stacey slurred out a few other words but mostly she just kept saying, "You're the bar pastor and you're in my bar."

She did say one other thing that stuck with me. She said, "I need to ask you about my daughter." I talked to Stacey for a little while and then went on my way, but I knew I had what I needed. I knew where she worked and that she wanted to talk to me about her daughter.

A few days later I decided to return to the bar, hoping to find Stacey at work. Sure enough, she was working and I could tell was she embarrassed when she saw me. I walked straight up to her and said, "Hey, Stacey, how are you doing?"

At that she let out a cussword and said, "I am so embarrassed. I was trashed the other night when I met you. I didn't say anything stupid, did I?"

I should have pulled a quick one on her and come up with a big story about what she said, but instead I just said, "No, you just told me that you worked here and that you needed to ask me something about your daughter. So tell me, what's up with your daughter?"

She skated around the question a little and then said, "She is just growing up. Maybe I'll connect with you later about her."

I could tell there was a lot more to it, but it wasn't the right time to talk, so I told her I'm always available if she wanted to talk more.

A few weeks later, I received a phone call at my church office. When I answered it, I could hear a woman on the other end holding back tears as she said, "Josh, this is Stacey from the bar. Can I come in and talk to you?"

I told her to come straight over and we could talk. Stacey sat down in my office and started into the deep, dark story of her daughter. She shared with me that her daughter had been going through drastic changes. It all started when her daughter started hanging out with a girl who was a couple of years older than her. This girl had influenced her daughter to deceive her mom, drink, steal, do drugs, and get involved sexually with her in a lesbian relationship. And Stacey's daughter was only eleven years old!

As she was telling me this story I felt like I was watching *Thirteen*. (*Thirteen* is a movie about a girl who gets led astray and manipulated by one of her friends.) Stacey said she knew some bad things were happening but that it finally came to a head the previous night. She said when she came home from work she found her daughter lying on her bed crying and continually repeating, "I'm so alone. I feel dark inside."

A Dark Hole

I talked to Stacey for a while about parenting and what to do about the situation, but then I told her that, more than anything, she and her daughter needed Jesus. I talked to her about why her daughter was feeling empty. I asked her if she had the same feelings, and she said yes. I told her we all have a place in our heart designed to be filled by God. It is as if we have a hole in our heart that Jesus is supposed to fill. He is the only one who can perfectly fill it. When we try to shove other things in it, it is like trying to shove a square peg into a round hole. It doesn't fit. I communicated to her that they both needed to quit searching after things that don't fit and instead surrender and try Jesus.

Zacchaeus suffered from this exact problem. He had a hole in his heart and he wanted it to be filled. Zacchaeus was a tax collector. That meant he was an outcast to most Jews. The tax collectors were hated because they worked for the Romans and were considered sinners for doing so. Think about the looks he got from people when he collected their taxes. Think about the words said underneath people's breath as he walked by. He was empty.

From his career, his friends, his admission of guilt, and his desire to see Jesus, we can tell Zacchaeus had a hole in his heart and was longing for it to be filled. He wanted to see Jesus so bad that when the crowds got too big, he climbed up in a tree. It was at that point that Jesus saw him and said, "Come down immediately. I must stay at your house today." He immediately came down out of the tree and repented of his life. Jesus replied by saying, "Today salvation has come to this house" (Luke 19:9). That day, Zacchaeus went from being empty to being full of God.

We also can see this in the story of the man out of whom Jesus cast demons in Luke 8:26–39. In this story, a man had become possessed by a multitude of demons. The demons actually called themselves "Legion" because many had gone into him. His demon possession had driven him mad to the point that the town counted him as dead. The townspeople chained him to the tombs in the cemetery. By doing so, they were insinuating that in their minds he was dead.

Can you imagine the people of your town casting you off as a dead person? Saying you no longer mattered? What would that do to your heart? You know this man had to feel extremely empty inside. Many times he broke free of the chains and ran around naked and screaming. And that's what he was like when Jesus met him. Jesus landed on the shore, and this demon-possessed man came running at him. Jesus stopped him in his tracks because the demons realized they were face to face with the Son of God. He cast out the demons and set the man free. I love what it says in verse 35: "They found the man from whom the demons had gone out, sitting at Jesus' feet, dressed, and in his right mind." That is such a perfect picture of what it means to go from feeling empty to having the hole in your heart filled. He was with Jesus, so he was no longer empty

Both of these stories do an excellent job of helping us to see what happens when we encounter Christ. He takes away the loneliness by filling the hole in our heart. Every one of us has tried at different times to fill the hole in our heart with the wrong things. We have tried to take care of the emptiness with the things of the world. We must realize Jesus is the only one who can fill the hole in our hearts. He is the only one who can fix our broken, cracked, and messed-up hearts. He can take care of the void. Therefore, go to him rather than other things.

Be willing to share this with people. Think about what both Zacchaeus and the demon-possessed man did. They both, after they met Jesus, turned to their friends and families and started sharing with them the fulfillment they found in Christ. Zacchaeus had a party, and the demon-possessed man started sharing Christ with his entire town. You are going to come in contact with people who feel empty. They feel empty because they are missing Jesus from their lives. They are trying to put a square peg in the round hole of their hearts. Be there and be ready to explain to people the only thing that can fill the hole, the only thing that can take care of the emptiness, is a relationship with Jesus.

Empty

QUESTIONS TO PONDER

What did you learn from Stacey's story?

When is a time you felt empty inside?

List ways you or others try to fill the hole in your/their heart.

Read the whole story of the woman at the well in John 4. What do you learn from her story?

The woman at the well filled the hole in her heart with Jesus, and then she went out and helped others fill their holes with Jesus as well. Sit silently with God right now and get filled up. Once you are full, go spill on people!

Scriptures to Study

1 Chronicles 28:9
Psalm 139
Romans 1:19–20
Psalm 63:1–5

Thoughts and Prayers

Spend some time journaling your thoughts about this chapter. What stuck out to you from the stories? How can you implement what you read into your life? Spend some time praying.

Prayer need: _____
Prayer need: _____
Prayer need: _____

Journal

Chapter Sixteen
This Is War

"This isn't a little game you are playing. This is war!"

For our struggle is not against flesh and blood, but against the rulers, against the authorities, against the powers of this dark world and against the spiritual forces of evil in the heavenly realms.

—Eph. 6:12

A Girl Named Ashley

A small country church in a rural little town wanted to have a big Christian rock concert. They wanted to get all of the kids from their town to come together to hear the message of Christ. They decided to have a large concert at the town park and make it as loud as they could. A band was invited to rock out and then play some worship music.

I was asked if I would attend and preach an evangelistic message after the worship. For a small country church, they were dreaming big and hoping kids would show up. And they did.

I was hanging out by the food area, munching some chips and drinking a Diet Coke, when Ashley came up. I greeted her and introduced myself. Our conversation went as follows:

"Hi, I'm Josh."

"I'm Ashley."

"Did you come here with any friends?"

"No."

"Do you go to the church that is putting this event on, or did you come with another church?"

"No, I don't go to church."

I followed up with a non-threatening question. "Well, what brought you here?"

"I live down the road and heard the loud music so I thought I would come see what was going on. Is it OK that I'm here?"

"Oh, yeah, it is great that you are here."

We continued to talk for a while. Eventually she spotted some girls she knew from school and went to hang out with them. I immediately started praying for Ashley and asking God to grab hold of her.

The Rain

As the band was rocking out, I noticed ugly-looking clouds starting to roll in. It was right as the band was going from some performance numbers into a worship set that it started to rain. It wasn't a nice little spring sprinkle. No, it was as if God had opened up the floodgates and let it pour.

The leader of the band gave me a questioning look as if saying, "Should we keep playing?" In turn, I looked to the youth minister who was putting on the event and asked him if we should keep going.

"As long as it isn't lightning, let's do this," he said.

So I looked back at the band's front man and gave him the hand signals to keep going. He just laughed. Then he spoke through the microphone and used a metaphor about how the rain was God's way of saying he was there...so let's dance with him.

With that, they started into some crazy, high-energy worship. Students were going nuts. Dancing. Shouting. Singing. I noticed the more they danced and the more it continued to rain, the area where they were standing was turning into pure mud. That didn't stop them. It only intensified what they were doing. These kids were having a blast dancing and worshiping the Lord and at the same time getting covered in mud. And Ashley was right in the midst of them.

When I eventually got on stage to preach, all I could see was teeth and eyes. All the kids close to the stage were totally covered in mud. The rain had stopped, and I asked them to sit down in the mud while I preached.

As I preached, I noticed two things. First, I realized the mud on the kids was starting to dry. The wind had picked up after the rain and it was drying out the once wet, smooth, good-feeling mud. Now it was starting to harden and crack as it clung to the students' bodies.

Second, I noticed Ashley, who was covered head to toe in mud, was sitting on the first row. I could only see her eyes because of all the mud, but it was enough to see God was moving her. I could tell by the look in Ashley's eyes God was grabbing hold of her and convicting her heart.

The Decision

As the sermon came to a close, I shared Jesus' parable of the prodigal son. I talked to them about the young man who left home and was living in sin. He was so down and out he was going through pigpens looking for food. I explained how one day, as he was down on his hands and knees covered in mud, he came to his senses and realized he needed his father. He decided it was time to go home. He had no idea what his father would say. He wasn't sure if his father would accept him back. All he knew was he needed his father.

I told the students he got up out of the mud and went to his father, in the same way they needed to get out of the mud and go to their father. I said to them, "You might not know everything about God, but all you need to know is you need him."

The band started to play, then I said a few more words. I could see big tears welling up in Ashley's eyes, and I knew she wanted to get out of the mud and give her life to Jesus. I started praying very hard that Ashley would have the strength to stand. I saw her put her hands down in the mud to help her stand. She wanted to stand and accept Christ, but there was a problem. She was stuck. Literally! The mud had dried around her, and I could tell she physically was having difficulty standing. I prayed for her to find the strength. I asked God to free her from the claws of Satan. Eventually, she broke free from the mud and came forward.

Ashley walked up to me and said words I'll never forget: "Josh, I don't know anything about Jesus, but I do know that I need him and want him."

"That's all you need to know," I said,

The Point

Ashley's story is a valuable lesson in evangelism. The first thing we learn is curiosity is a wonderful thing. Think about it. People always want to know stuff, such as "What's in the box?" or "What did she say?" or "What is going on over there?" Ashley came to the event simply because of curiosity. She heard the music and wondered what was going on. As Christians, we often forget curiosity can be a great evangelism tool. I can't tell you how many times people have asked me questions because they were curious about something I was doing. Your life should look different than everyone else's. If your life is different, people will want to know why. We need to take hold of people's curiosity and show them the way. Answer their questions. 1 Peter 3:15 says, "Always be prepared to give a reason for your hope." Do things in your life and live in such a way that people are curious about you. Their curiosity will open doors for evangelism.

Second, it is extremely hard to accept Jesus when your sin and Satan hold you back. You must be willing to rise up out of the mud pit. Think about the friends with whom you are trying to share your faith. How much mud (sin) are they sitting in? How thick is it? If they are sitting very deep in the mud, it is going to be difficult for them to break free, to stand up. It is as if the mud has hold of them. And it isn't just the mud/sin that has them in captivity, it is also Satan.

As I look back on that day when Ashley was trying to stand up but couldn't because she was stuck, I remember spiritually thinking it was as if Satan had reached up through the ground and was holding her back with his nasty hands. I recall praying for God to rebuke Satan and to release his grip. Satan has his claws on your friends and family. This isn't a little game you are playing. This is war! You are in a battle for the souls of your friends. Ephesians 6:12 says, "For our struggle is not against flesh and blood, but against the rulers, against the authorities, against the powers of this dark world and against the spiritual forces of evil in the heavenly realms." That is reality. This isn't make believe. Demons are real! Satan is real! There is a spiritual war taking place right around us. There are spiritual battles happening all the time for our souls.

Every time you start to share your faith with a non-Christian, you can bet a spiritual force of evil reaches up and holds down the nonbeliever. The mud gets thick! It makes it difficult for a person to come to Christ, but not impossible. Romans 8:37–39 says, "No, in all these things we are more than conquerors through him who loved us. For I am convinced that neither death nor life, neither angels nor demons, neither the present nor the future, nor any powers, neither height nor depth, nor anything else in all creation, will be able to separate us from the love of God that is in Christ Jesus our Lord." Again, this isn't an impossible battle. Paul says in Romans nothing can separate us from God's love. His love wins. Therefore, go, share his love, and win the war.

Third, Ashley's story teaches us people don't have to have all the answers to accept Jesus. Ashley didn't know the whole creation story. She hadn't heard about the deity of Christ. She hadn't studied all of his miracles. She hadn't even read the Bible. What she heard was she was a sinner who needed to be saved; and, in her case, that was all she needed to hear. Her words were simple: "I don't know anything about Jesus, but I do know that I need him." That is all someone needs to know. Therefore, when you are sharing your faith, don't assume people have to have all the answers. Don't try to teach them the entire Bible or let them get sidetracked on unimportant issues. Keep the conversation focused on Jesus and our desperate need for him to save us.

QUESTIONS TO PONDER

What did you learn from Ashley's story?

What can you do today that will raise someone's curiosity about you and your faith?

Are you still sitting in mud? If so, spend some time repenting and allow God to cleanse you.

What comes to your mind when you think about spiritual warfare? How do you fight that battle? Read Ephesians 6:10–20. Find someone who will be an Ephesians 6:19–20 prayer warrior for you.

Scriptures to Study

James 4:7
Ephesians 6:10–24
Luke 4:1–13
Luke 23:39–43

Thoughts and Prayers

Spend some time journaling your thoughts about this chapter. What stuck out to you from the stories? How can you implement what you read into your life? When you are finished journaling, take some time to pray.

Prayer need: _____
Prayer need: _____
Prayer need: _____

Journal

Chapter Seventeen
Help for the Hurting

"You can't help a hurting person with a bulldozer—you must do it with a shovel"

Blessed are those that mourn, for they will be comforted.

—Matt. 5:4

James

He broke the rules. There is a set of rules every guy knows exists and he broke them. It was a Saturday night, and my wife and I had gone to Wal-Mart to do some grocery shopping. While we were there I went to the bathroom. I was standing at the urinal when James came in and broke the rules.

The rules of the urinal are simple:

1. You don't choose the urinal next to someone if there are others available.
2. You step up to the plate and look at the wall.
3. You never, ever, talk.

James violated every one of these rules. He came in, stood at the urinal next to me, and looked at me right in the eyes as he introduced himself. Obviously, I was a little taken aback and surprised by his introduction, but that didn't stop him. He just continued talking while I was taking care of business. He ended up telling me he had been at our church service that night and wanted to talk with me a little. We talked for a bit and then I encouraged him to come by my office (a much more appropriate place) and we could talk some more.

On Monday, James showed up and asked if we could talk. We went back to my office and started sharing with one another. James told me he was very depressed and an alcoholic. Then he did something that freaked me out a little. He started to take off his shirt and asked, "Do you mind if I show you something?"

When he took off his shirt, I couldn't believe what I saw. James's chest and arms were covered with scars. He had burned all the skin off of one shoulder, and he had dug a hole in his other shoulder with razor blades. In addition, he had sliced open every inch of his chest.

James showed me the biggest scar and went on to tell me about the night it had happened. He said he was living by himself because his wife had left him. When he came home from work he was terribly depressed, so he picked up a bottle and drank until the liquor was gone. From there he decided his life wasn't worth living. He had cut himself many times before, but this time he wanted to do more than just cut himself, he wanted to kill himself.

He pulled out his blade and started cutting, and then with one stroke he pushed it deeper than he ever had before and pulled it across his chest. With that stroke, he prayed, "God, if you want me to live, then you make it happen," and then he passed out in his own blood.

For some unknown reason, his next-door neighbor came over the next morning and through the window saw James lying in his own blood. The neighbor immediately called 911, and they rushed James to the hospital. A doctor there patched him up and saved his life. Or, I should say, God saved his life.

I expected after hearing his testimony James was going to tell me how thankful he was God had saved his life that day and how he now found fulfillment in God. Unfortunately, what he told me was he wished he had died that day. He said his life was no better today than it was then. He confessed he still drank, still cut himself, and was still lonely and depressed daily.

A Commitment to Love

I talked with James for a while in my office that day. I convinced him to try to give God a chance. I asked him if he would come back the next week and allow me to connect him with some other Christians. The next Sunday, he showed up, and I introduced him to some other folks who have been through tough times.

James was struggling with depression, addictions, and pain. He was hurting and needed help. You come in contact with hurting people all the time: friends whose parents are breaking up, a guy who is addicted to meth, a church member who is dying, a family member who is depressed, a classmate who has an eating disorder, or a girl who is cutting.

Most teenagers know someone who is cutting. Cutting has become an addiction for many teens. You notice I used the word *addiction* because that is what it is. I've talked to several cutters, and each one said he or she was addicted to it because the physical pain was easier to deal with than the mental pain. These cutters said they had tried to stop, but every time they got depressed they found themselves grabbing for a blade.

Helping hurting people is a very difficult thing to do because there isn't an easy, overnight fix. Most hurting people are dealing with depression and a lack of self-esteem, two issues that take a long time to fix. It is a long process that requires a lot of time, energy, prayer, people, and an active commitment. People can be hurting because all of the sudden the rug was pulled out from other them—parents split, someone dies, etc. But most of the time people are hurting because thing after thing has piled up over time. When this happens, the hurting person gets trapped underneath a pile of pain. In order to help these types of people, you must be willing to love them, and love them, and love them, no matter how much work it is. You can't help a hurting person with a bulldozer—you must do it with a shovel. Are you willing to commit to love them?

Help for the Hurting

Tyler found Christians with that kind of commitment. Tyler was a student in my student ministry who struggled with self-esteem, depression, and his purpose in life. During his junior year of high school, he tried to commit suicide. After his unsuccessful attempt, he wrote this letter:

> For all of you that don't know, in February I tried to kill myself. I blame it on the crappy world we live in. I tried to kill myself for a lot of reasons. One reason was because I was lonely. I wasn't good enough for anyone, I cried almost every night. I started isolating myself because I didn't want to make anyone else unhappy. I tried to kill myself by cutting my wrist because I thought death had to be better than this crappy world we live in. I have a teacher in school who always tells us life isn't fair and we need to learn that. I think he is full of crap. The only reason life isn't fair is because people have stopped caring. There is a song that says, I looked at the guy next to me, he didn't look too happy, no one's happy, but we're all too busy to see. Now I think some people are happy, but I also think people need to look around and open their eyes and see those people hurting inside and go over and talk to them because you care, not because you pity them. No one wants pity. Everyone just wants a little love.

Tyler was a young man who needed love. Thankfully, some students in my church made an active commitment to love him and give him God. It is difficult to stay committed to such a task, but with the strength of God you can keep someone's life alive and give him or her joy. Isaiah 61:1 says, "The Spirit of the Sovereign Lord is on me, because the Lord has anointed me…He has sent me to bind up the brokenhearted." You have the Spirit of the almighty God upon you. You have the power to help change a life. Yes, it is difficult. Yes, it takes a lot of love and a huge commitment, but you can do it because you have been anointed by God to do it. Isaiah 61:3 says when you bind up the brokenhearted you give them the oil of gladness instead of mourning. You need to give them God so their eyes can be filled with joy instead of tears. They might still hurt, but through God they can find joy in the midst of their pain.

Are You Committed or Just Playing?

I'm happy to say I ran into Tyler not long ago, and he told me he is feeling better than he ever has before. He also told me he is now a youth pastor and spends his time helping people. His is a success story because people made an active commitment to loving him. Unfortunately, that isn't always the case. Many times it takes too much work and people won't make the commitment.

I thought James was getting plugged in to our church. But I found out differently. I got a letter from him that convicted me to write this chapter. His letter read, "I hear your church is doing well and is growing, but I'm still lost. I still drink every day, stick razor blades in my arms and lighters to my chest, and have shame in my heart. I'm glad you are growing, but I am dying."

Are you committed or are you just playing?

Questions to Ponder

What did you learn from James's story?

Whom do you know who is cutting, throwing up, going through pain, and/or hurting?

How can you help them?

What did you learn from the difference between James and Tyler?

Pray for James right now.

Scriptures to Study

Romans 12:15
John 5:1–9
James 5:13–16
Colossians 3:12–17

Thoughts and Prayers

Spend some time journaling your thoughts about this chapter. What stuck out to you from the stories? How can you implement what you read into your life? Spend some time praying.

Prayer need: _____
Prayer need: _____
Prayer need: _____

Journal

Chapter Eighteen

Family

"Don't be afraid to get uncomfortable—it is an essential element of sharing your faith."

Honor your father and your mother.
—Ex. 20:12

Fran and Mike

Fran and Mike might be the hardest people with whom I've ever had to share my faith. Most of the time I felt like I was supposed to say something, but I was too chicken. When I did get the courage to say something, it just felt wrong. I would stumble through my words or feel wrong for confronting Fran and Mike, or they would show me how my life didn't match up to my words.

They knew the true Josh and made sure I knew that. You see, Fran and Mike are my parents.

As I said previously, I didn't grow up in the church. I attended a couple of times as a kid, but that was it. My mom, dad, and brother didn't attend church either. My mom, Fran, grew up in the church. Her dad was an elder in a church on the south side of Indianapolis. She grew up going to church every Sunday and going to camp in the summer, but as she got older she walked away from her faith.

My stepdad, Mike, had a little different story. He attended church off and on as a kid, but it wasn't until he was an adult that he really heard the message of God. When I was in junior high school he got turned on to God and gave his life to him, but unfortunately it didn't stick at that time.

Mike was a perfect example of the story found in Mark 4 about the sower and the seed. Mike was like the rocky place. He accepted the seed but, because he didn't have any roots, he fell away. My older brother, Jack, was not a believer either. He landed a job right out of high school because of his intelligence, and it paid him extremely well. He was bringing in more money than I could imagine and was using it to enjoy life. It seemed like every other weekend he was heading off on some extreme trip—Utah to climb mountains, the Caribbean to go snorkeling, or Colorado to go skiing. When he wasn't traveling, he was playing in clubs around Indy in a rock-and-roll band. He had a life most young men dream about; therefore, he thought he had no need for God.

When I turned my life over to Christ my senior year of high school, I immediately felt the need to share my faith with my family. I wanted them to find the same God I had found. I wanted them to feel the love and peace I was now feeling, so I started looking for opportunities to share my faith. Unfortunately, I didn't do a very good job at first because of my fear, ignorance, and lifestyle at home.

Sharing your faith with your family members is by far the hardest. I think it is extremely difficult for a couple of reasons. One, all your life you have followed the instructions of your parents. From the time you are born they tell you what you should and shouldn't do to make it through life. They are the teachers, and you are the student. When you try to tell them about God, you are reversing roles. You become the teacher and they become the student. You have to confront them on their lifestyle. You have to tell them of their need for Jesus. You have to share with them the consequences of a bad decision. It is a role reversal and an extremely difficult one.

Second, I think it is difficult because they know your faults. They know everything about you. About four months after I became a Christian I was trying to talk to my mom about Christ and about my wanting to go to Cincinnati Christian University. The conversation ended when she said, "You say that Jesus has changed your life and that you are totally different now than before. Well, maybe you are different when you are away from home, but I haven't seen a bit of difference inside this house." When she said that, it cut me to the heart and I couldn't argue with her. Had I been going the extra mile to serve my parents? Had I sat in the living room reading my

Bible? Had I kept my room clean? Had I even taken out the trash without hesitation when asked? My life had changed outside of the walls of my home. But nothing had changed inside my house, and for that I had to repent. If you want to bring your family to Christ, it starts by how you live at home. Witnessing to your family is extremely difficult; but through love, life change, prayer, and patience, you can bring them to Christ.

Love

It starts with love. You have to let the love that is in your heart for your family consume you. If you truly love them, then your heart will break for their lost souls and will convict you to persist in sharing your faith. Without love you won't be up to the task because of how difficult it can be. But with love you will do whatever it takes to share your faith. Whatever it takes means giving up time with your friends so you can spend time with your family. It means waking up early so you can talk to your dad before he leaves for work. It means getting out of your comfort zone.

I wanted to share my faith with my dad but wasn't able to get the words out of my mouth. I just didn't feel comfortable enough with my dad to talk to him about Christ. My dad and I didn't talk much. One, he was my stepdad, and two, he is quiet by nature. Now, don't get me wrong, we had a great relationship. I knew he deeply loved me and cared for me, we just didn't say that to one another. We talked about sports and cars and that was the extent of it. Goodbyes and goodnights were verbal, not physical. So to talk to my dad about spiritual things # Family

just didn't seem to happen. I tried many different ways to get the conversation started, but none of them ever came out of my mouth.

This went on for a couple of years, and then I finally decided the best place to start with my dad was through love. I knew if I didn't show him I loved him that I wouldn't be able to tell him Jesus loved him. So I made the decision that I would verbally tell him I loved him and hug him. I still remember the first hug. I hadn't seen him or my mom for a couple of months, so we met up one night for dinner. When we finished eating dinner and were standing in the parking lot saying goodbye, my mom hugged me. When she finished hugging me I walked over to my dad and hugged him and told him I loved him. I know it caught him off guard and made him feel extremely uncomfortable, and me as well, but it was so needed. By getting out of our comfort zones that night and many times since, it has opened up other areas where we are willing to get uncomfortable. Don't be afraid to get uncomfortable. It is an essential element in sharing your faith.

Life Change

Life change is an essential element if you want to share your faith with your family. They know the true you—that can be good or bad. If the true you is good, then that's good. If the true you is bad, then change!

As I said earlier, my mom knew the true me. Inside the house I hadn't changed. I made a conscious decision that day to change my entire life. I started living differently inside the house. I wanted to make sure my mom could never make that statement again. About six months after our initial conversation about my wanting to go to Cincinnati Christian University we talked about it again. This time my mom ended the conversation by saying, "Your life change is very evident to me now, and I will do whatever I can to help you go to that school." My life change had won over my mom. It hadn't won her over to accepting Christ, but it had softened her heart to the gospel.

If you want to share your faith with your family, then make sure you are living your faith in front of them. It is very difficult because you must be conscious of your actions one-hundred-percent of the time, but without life change you have no leg to stand on. Do everything in your power to live the life of Christ in front of your family. The way you talk, serve, study, pray, love, etc. is a reflection of your faith in God.

Prayer

Another thing you must be willing to do if you want your family to come to Christ is to pray for them. Pray without ceasing for the salvation of your family. Because it can be so difficult to save your family, you must rely on the power of prayer.

I especially prayed for my brother. I was bothered that I couldn't share my faith with him. One of the major reasons why is we never saw one another. We were living in different cities, and he was working and going off on exotic trips while I was going to school. The only thing I could do was pray for him. So I did that a lot.

One day my prayer was answered in the form of a girl named Allisa. My brother started dating Allisa and they ended up getting married. Allisa had grown up in church, and shortly after they were married she talked him into going to church. He has since accepted Christ and is a very active youth coach at his church.

Did I have a huge part in my brother finding God? I believe my prayers did. I prayed that somehow my brother would come to Christ, and he did. God brought a girl into his life who was willing to share her faith. So many times people think they have to be the one who brings a person to Christ. Remember there are a lot of people out there working for the King. Many times you simply need to pray for a worker to come in contact with the person for whom you are praying.

Patience

Patience is the last thing you must have when it comes to your family. Chances are your family isn't going to come to Christ overnight, but rather it is going to take a long time.

It took ten years before my mom and dad came back to Christ. There were many times I thought it would never happen, but I wasn't going to give up. I was patient and kept looking for ways to get them in contact with God. A lot of times it was little things. When I was preaching at a church close to Indy I would invite my mom and dad to come. If my kids were in a program at church I would invite them to come see their grandkids perform. I would drop little comments about Christ or the church into conversations. I didn't force-feed them or pressure them. I just took baby steps, and eventually they took steps with me.

I remember the night I believe my parents returned to their faith. It was in October 1999. My mom and dad called and asked if I could meet them for dinner. We met at a Chinese buffet in Avon, Indiana.

The conversation started quickly when they asked me, "Josh, do you think Jesus will return or that the world will end at midnight on New Year's Eve?"

You see, there was a big scare called "Y2K" going on all around the world. Many people believed that when midnight hit and the year 2000 began, all the computers in the world were going to crash and that the world was going to be destroyed. Some illiterate Bible teachers also taught that Jesus would return at the same time, ushering in the end of the world.

In preparation for this threat, many people had started collecting canned goods, water, power generators, etc. My parents were part of that group. Their basement was full of food and water.

Theirs was an honest question I was more than willing to answer. I replied, "I don't know."

I continued by saying, "I have no clue when Jesus will return. It could be that night, it could be three hundred years from now, or it could be tonight. Jesus said he will come like a thief in the night. No one can predict the night of his return; therefore we must be ready every night."

We went on to talk a lot more that night, and I ended the conversation by asking them, "Are you ready if he returns tonight?" That conversation turned the corner for them, and since then they have returned to their faith. I thank the Lord daily for their faith. If it weren't for patience, I would have given up. Don't ever give up. Instead, be persistent and patient.

Jesus

Lastly, on days when you are weary because your family doesn't believe, remember Jesus. He is the Son of God. He was born of a virgin. He changed the water to wine, fed the fish to the five thousand, healed the mouth of a mute, and made the legs work of the lame. He walked on water, blessed the blind, loved the leper, delivered the demon-possessed, and called forth the dead. He turned over the tables in the temple, tore down the traditions of time, and tore into the teachers of the law. He hated religion, yet loved relationships. He talked with tax collectors and partied with prostitutes, yet his family didn't believe in him. His mother followed from a distance, and his brothers tried to send him away (John 7:5). There will be days when you feel like giving up. Focus on Christ and on how difficult it must have been for him. He didn't give up but instead saved our souls and the souls of his family. His brother James went from being a nonbeliever to being one of the leaders in the early church. Stay the course.

QUESTIONS TO PONDER

What did you learn from Fran, Mike, and Jack?
List your family members who don't believe.
Have you been showing them love? How have you gotten or how can you get out of your comfort zone with them?

Have you had a life change inside your home? What can you do better inside the walls of your house and in front of your family to show them your life change and faith?

Be patient and pray.

Scriptures to Study

Ephesians 6:1–3
Matthew 10:35–39
2 Peter 3:9
2 Corinthians 5:17–20

Thoughts and Prayers

Spend some time journaling your thoughts about this chapter. What stuck out to you from the stories? How can you implement what you read into your life? Spend some time praying.

Prayer need: _____
Prayer need: _____
Prayer need: _____

Journal

Chapter Nineteen
Contagious Worship

"Worship is one of the most evangelistic things you can do, because it is contagious."

Come, let us bow down in worship.

—Ps. 95:6

The Earthquake in Cincinnati

"By the city of Covington, Kentucky, you are no longer permitted to do that song."

Those were the words spoken by a police officer who grabbed a microphone at a conference I was attending.

It was the opening night of a conference for junior high school students. Over two thousand people had gathered in Covington, Kentucky (just across the river from Cincinnati), for this conference. As the crowd started to come into the second-floor ballroom of the convention center, you could feel the excitement in the air. When the band started into the first number, the crowd went wild and started celebrating. After the first song, the band's front man addressed the crowd and said, "We are here to worship God, so don't hold back. Give him everything you've got!" And that they did!

What happened next still blows my mind. The band started playing a song that had a dance routine between the verses and the chorus. Everyone in the audience knew the dance moves. When that part of the song hit and everyone jumped to the right at the exact same time, I took notice. I noticed, because I had been sitting on the floor backstage and I was now airborne. With over two thousand people jumping at once it was causing the floor to give, and it bounced a full six inches. Immediately got up, looked out at the crowd, and saw our screens swaying and our sound techs trying to hold their soundboards to the table.

But the funniest thing was yet to come.

I started to run to the back of the room. As I got there, I saw the building supervisor coming through the ballroom doors just as the band was getting to the dancing part of the song again. When the kids jumped, they caused the floor to bounce so drastically that the air was pushed out of the room, causing the building supervisor's hair to get blown straight back on end.

She quickly asked me, "What are you guys doing?"

I replied, "Dancing."

It was right then that the police officer grabbed the microphone. I got the crowd calmed down and told them what had happened. I told them to worship, but they couldn't dance. I hated telling them that, but I had to because they weren't just causing the floor to bounce, they were causing the drywall to crack and the ceiling tiles to fall on the convention center workers.

I found out later mass panic had broken out among the crowd on the first floor during the dancing song. There were people attending another event on that level. When the building swayed, they all had run out into the streets screaming, "Earthquake!"

Hope in Haiti

Devastation, despair, discouragement, poverty, dirt, voodoo, and sin. In the midst of all that, it is joy I saw in the hearts and on the faces of Haitian children.

I was in Haiti on a mission trip with Compassion International. While I was there, I was blown away by the extreme poverty I saw. I saw handicapped children with no help, homes that sheltered ten people with only two rooms, children with bloated bellies, and families with no food or water. I had never witnessed such devastation, but I also have to admit I had never witnessed so much joy. When our group arrived at a children's project, all of the children ran out to our vehicles and start clapping, cheering, and shouting. They were exhilarated that we were there. We often played with the kids for an hour or so, and then they would put on a program for us.

My favorite part of the program was always the worship. I loved it because all the kids would sing at the tops of their lungs. The volume was intense, and their smiles were contagious. Every time they would finish a song, I would ask them to sing another one. When those kids were singing you could tell they had forgotten their poverty. The only thing they needed was to be in the presence of the Lord. They went there and took me along as well.

No Singing in Nashville

It was the night I couldn't sing. Oh, I worshiped like I had never worshiped before, but I did so without opening my mouth.

I was at a retreat for about sixty artists and speakers at a famous musician's farm in Nashville. Being an artist/speaker is very exciting, but it also can be very difficult. You are constantly on the road, surrounded by people and away from your family. It's not just physically and emotionally demanding, it's spiritually demanding. It can be very difficult to find times of refreshment with the Lord. We were all at this retreat so we could find that refreshment. I was looking forward to a couple of days just spending time in his Word and worshiping him.

As the worship leader started leading the singing, I jumped right in and started belting out the lyrics. Now you must understand, I'm not a singer. I love to sing, but God didn't gift me with a favorable voice. As I was singing, I started to hear some things I don't normally hear during worship. I was hearing not just the melody, but harmonies, parts, soul, and much more. I was surrounded by some of the best voices in Christian music: Bebo Norman, Alathea, Rachael Lampa, Caedmon's Call, Acapella, Geoff Moore, Phil Keaggy, Randy Stonehill, Buddy Greene, and on and on and on. At that moment there was no way I could continue to sing. I didn't want to ruin the beautiful blend of voices I was hearing. I didn't sing, but, oh, did I worship. I allowed my mind and heart to be carried to the throne of God by the voices and worship happening around me.

What Does Worship Have to Do with Evangelism?

I know what you are probably thinking right now: why is this chapter on worship? It's an honest question because most of the time people don't think worship and evangelism have anything to do with one another. Most people would say non-Christians can't worship because they don't have a relationship with God. The truth is, worship is one of the most evangelistic things you can possibly do. When people see you worshiping they will want to jump in. That is why worship and evangelism go hand in hand. Because of this, it is crucial to understand what worship is. It is critical to learn to engage in worship. It is an essential element of evangelism. Worship is one of the most evangelistic things you can do, because it is contagious.

King David shows us worship is evangelistic in 2 Samuel 6. The Bible records that David went to the house of Obed Edom to get the ark of the covenant to bring it back to Jerusalem. After he took six steps with the ark, he then stopped to offer a sacrifice to God. From there he broke out into intense worship to the point that it says in verse 14 he "danced before the Lord with all his might wearing his linen ephod." His ephod, in basic terms, means his underwear. David was dancing around in his underwear, praising God at the top of his lungs. He was dancing violently as an act of worship. He didn't allow his pride to get in the way and make him act prim and proper. Instead, he humbled himself before the Lord and gave God everything he had. Because of it, people noticed. It is recorded in verse 15 that the whole house of Israel praised God with shouts and the playing of trumpets. It also states in verse 19 that a crowd had gathered around. People saw David and the crowd and became curious about what was going on. Some joined in the celebration and some, namely his wife, chose to abstain from the worship. David, through his worship, was able to get people connected to God.

Let's Dance

We must learn from David's example and put it into practice. When you worship in an authentic way, people take notice. Too many times I see people bring their friends to worship services and then do nothing to connect them to God. The most important thing you can do if you bring a friend to church with you is worship in an authentic way. If it is a time of celebration, then dance. If it is a time of repentance, then get on your knees. If it is a time to have a broken heart, then let it happen.

Authentic worship testifies to the person next to you that you not only believe in God, but you have a passion for him. I know sometimes you might not feel

Contagious Worship

like worshiping, but you have a responsibility to the person next to you. In the same way, people often allow their pride to get in the way. They are too cool to jump or too stubborn to raise their hands. That is a prideful attitude that must be erased through humility. Worship the Lord in an authentic and humble way so your friends will want to do the same.

Questions to Ponder

What did you learn from the Cincinnati story?
What did you learn from the Haiti story?
What did you learn from the Nashville story?
What did David teach you?

Does your worship take others to God or away from him? Does your pride keep you from being real with God? What type of effect does pride have on those who are non-Christians?

Scriptures to Study

Psalm 96:1–4
Psalm 100
Romans 12:1–2
John 4:21–24

Thoughts and Prayers

Spend some time journaling your thoughts about this chapter. What stuck out to you from the stories? How can you implement what you read into your life? Take time to pray.

Prayer need: _____
Prayer need: _____
Prayer need: _____

Journal

_____

_____

Chapter Twenty

Missed Opportunities

"That night a soul was hanging in the balance, and I failed to help her find God."

And how can they hear without someone preaching to them.

—Rom. 10:14

Amy

It was late one night and I was in the middle of nowhere Oklahoma. A worship band and I had been doing a concert. We wanted to grab a bite to eat before we headed back to the hotel, so we pulled in to my favorite restaurant, Chili's. What happened over the next hour saddened and convicted me.

We sat down at a table in Chili's and our waitress, Amy, came up and greeted us. Immediately she realized we weren't from around there. I don't know if it was the absence of an accent or the lack of belt buckles and cowboy hats, or simply the big bus that gave it away.

As she took our orders and served our food, Amy started asking us all kinds of questions. She asked us about our jobs and the concert we had just put on. In the process, she began to share her heart and her life, all while waiting on our table and those around us. Honestly, I have to admit I answered her questions, but I failed to engage her. I didn't intentionally ignore her or pass her off, but I by no means took our conversation to the next level. I was too concerned about eating and getting to bed.

It was only when I got out to the bus that I realized I had messed up. As I sat down and looked back at the restaurant, I saw Amy standing in the window. She just stood there and watched us pull off. It was in that precise moment that God slapped me upside the head and said, "You blew it." When I saw her standing there I realized I had just missed an opportunity to share Christ with her. Waitresses just don't stand around and look out windows!

I drove the bus to the hotel with tears streaming down my face. I walked straight up to my room, lay down, wept, and repented. I cried myself to sleep that night because I missed an opportunity to free a soul.

The Gravity of the Situation

I know that is a very short story, as it was a short encounter that night at Chili's, but understand the depth

Missed Opportunities

of what happened. Grasp how big a deal it is when you miss opportunities. Comprehend the gravity of it all, the weight and seriousness of it. You are dealing with the souls of individuals.

God gave me a task that night. He called me to share the gospel with Amy, and I failed. I failed to mention his name. I failed to help her find freedom in Christ. I failed to release her from the darkness. When you miss an opportunity, you can't just shrug it off as, "Oh, well." Amy might have died in a car wreck that night. She might have been contemplating suicide that night. She might have been ready to accept Christ that night because someone else had planted seeds that were ready to bloom.

Do you get it? That night, a soul was hanging in the balance, and I failed to help her find God. That is something that breaks my heart and leads me to repentance every time it happens.

The best way to guard against missed opportunities is to put Colossians 4:3–6 into practice: "And pray for us, too, that God may open a door for our message, so that we may proclaim the mystery of Christ, for which I am in chains. Pray that I may proclaim it clearly, as I should. Be wise in the way you act toward outsiders; make the most of every opportunity. Let your conversation be always full of grace, seasoned with salt, so that you may know how to answer everyone."

It starts with prayer. You must pray God will open doors for you to share your faith. You need to wake up every morning and ask God to bring someone into your life so you can share your faith. Think about it. If you ask God to place someone in your path, don't you think he will do it? First Timothy 2:4 says he wants all men to be saved and to come to a knowledge of the truth. If you pray that he opens the door for you to share your faith, then he will.

Pray also that you will be ready when he opens the door. Ask that you always will have your eyes open for possible opportunities. In addition, pray you will be able to share the mysteries of Christ with clarity. When you are given an opportunity, you don't want to blow it. Therefore, pray every day that God will open a door, that you will walk through it, and that you will proclaim his Word clearly.

Second, be wise how you talk and interact with other people. The Bible uses the word *outsiders.* Outsiders are those who are outside of the will of God. Most times you will have no idea if someone is a Christian or not. Therefore, you must treat everyone properly and with love. How is it possible to lead someone to Christ after you have been sinning with him or her through words or actions? You must act godly in front of them so you don't shut the door God is trying to open.

Third, make the most out of every opportunity. I didn't make the most of the opportunity I had with Amy that night. I passed by the open door, the encounter God placed in front of me. You must take advantage of every opportunity you get because you aren't guaranteed another chance will come tomorrow. Look for opportunities in the lunchroom, on the bus as you are heading to a game, passing periods between classes, and eating after a movie. There are so many opportunities every day we walk right past. Don't miss these open-door opportunities! Make the most of them!

Last, the Colossians 4:3–6 passage concludes by saying to make sure your conversation is full of grace so you will know how to answer people. The best way for me to explain this is don't judge through your conversation or try to debate. I've never seen someone come to Christ through a debate, but I've witnessed thousands of people accept Christ through love. One day I was in Atlanta with some students doing street evangelism, and a couple of my students started debating with a homeless man about the lordship of Christ. By arguing with him they didn't do anything for his faith. All they managed to do was get stumped by his questions. When you debate, you will lose. When you love and give grace, you will be able to answer people's questions.

I missed my chance with Amy because I wasn't prayed up and I didn't make the most of every opportunity. Because of that I wasn't able to answer her questions. I distinctly remember that night and the heaviness I felt because I didn't share my faith. I never want to feel that feeling again. Therefore, I must be ready. What about you?

QUESTIONS TO PONDER

What did you learn from Amy's story?

What opportunities have you missed lately?

How are you doing with your prayer life? Are you praying every day for open-door opportunities? Are you praying for clarity as you share your faith with others?

Are you being wise? Are you living a life that points people to Christ or away from him? List some times lately where you have failed to be wise in front of outsiders. What can you learn from each situation? How can you keep from repeating your unwise choice?

List some times, places, and people where you know you need to make the most of the opportunity God gives you.

Scriptures to Study

Matthew 25:1–13
Matthew 5:13–16
Acts 8:26–40

Thoughts and Prayers

Spend some time journaling your thoughts about this chapter. What stuck out to you from the stories that were told? How can you implement what you read into your life? When you are finished journaling, take some time to pray.

Prayer need: _____
Prayer need: _____
Prayer need: _____

Journal

Chapter Twenty-One
The Journey

"My destination is simply the celebrating point of my journey."

Follow me.

—Luke 5:27

My Spiritual Journey

One thing I have learned in life is everyone has to go through storms, whether it is a family breakup, cancer, a car wreck, or something else. Storms are the unseen things that happen to change your life.

In October 2003, my family was hit by a storm. It totally uprooted my life. It was one of those storms that made me question everything about my life, my faith, and my calling. After talking with my wife, she recommended I take a few days to go retreat with God. I decided to take her advice and go on a spiritual journey.

I didn't have a set agenda, but I had two places I needed to go: Nashville, Tennessee, and Las Vegas, Nevada. I decided to take a week, drive down to Nashville, drive across the southern United States, and then eventually end up in Las Vegas. I knew driving would be a huge retreat for me because it would allow me to spend some time in silence and in prayer.

I took the rear seats out of my minivan and made a bed in the back. For the next week, it would be my van, the road, my Bible, my journal, and me. I wasn't on a time schedule. Rather, I was just on a journey. I learned some things on my journey that still refresh me today. Maybe they will refresh you as well. This was one of the deepest weeks of my life.

The Creek

The first place I stopped was at a friend's house in Nashville. He is a speaker as well and was on the road, so I had his place all to myself. After a refreshing shower, I went out and sat beside a creek that runs through his backyard. For several hours I disappeared into a spiritual place with God. Trees, a quiet breeze, and falling leaves surrounded me. The subtle sounds of the creek provided me with an opportunity to drift away with God. I spent a lot of time reading my Bible and writing in my journal. I honestly can't tell you anything I read that day, but I can tell you it was one of the most refreshing times of my life. It was as if time was standing still so I could spend some quiet moments with God.

Many times since that day I have longed for that quiet place, that moment in time, that peaceful feeling. I long for that time at the creek, but I can't find it—my life is way too busy. I have to admit, most days I'm trying to squeeze God into a five-minute time slot in the morning.

I believe time is one of the biggest issues we face today. People are busier now than they have ever been before. I remember being busy in high school, but if I look at my life then to what an average high school student is involved with now, there is no comparison. Students are extremely busy. As I write this, I know my son's schedule today has him going from seven-thirty in the morning until nine tonight with only thirty minutes of down time—and he is only in fifth grade! It only gets worse as you get older. Because of this, many people are missing out—missing out on life, missing out on being a kid, and missing out on a vibrant relationship with God. When time is an issue, most people will cast off God first. This leads people to fall away from God, to get dry in their faith, and to become stagnant and empty.

So how can you share your faith with people when you are empty? You must find "time at the creek" so you can share your faith out of that overflow of your spiritual life, not from the bottom. Psalm 46:10 says, "Be still and know that I am God." Psalm 5:3 says, "In the morning, O Lord, you hear my voice; in the morning I lay my requests before you and wait in expectation." Find some time to spend "at the creek" every day so your faith will be vibrant and you will overflow on people.

Sleeping

Each day I drove as far as I could until I was just too tired to go on. At that point I pulled over at the next exit, crawled into the back of my van, and went to sleep. At first I thought this would be simple: I had a mattress, a pillow, a blanket, and everything needed to get a great night's sleep. After the first night I realized how hard it was to sleep like that. I was startled easily and woke up at every noise around me. In addition, by the early morning hours I was always freezing. I thought I would sleep like a baby! Well, in reality I did: I woke up every hour, looked around, got back in the fetal position to get warm, and fell back asleep.

My car is not the only place I've slept that is a little unusual. I've also slept on sidewalks and in city parks. One day while I was in St. Louis, I had an hour to kill, so I just stretched out on the sidewalk and took a nap. When I first laid down I noticed a lot of people staring at me, as if I was homeless, but not stopping to help.

I've also taken a lot of naps in many city parks. I once laid down in a park in Atlanta. This particular park was a major hangout for homeless men, so people sleeping on the grass was common. I saw a bunch of men sleeping and I thought it looked inviting, so I did the same thing. I don't know if the homeless men in the park that day respected me for sleeping there, but I noticed when I woke up and started talking to them it was as if we had a kindred spirit.

I've also slept on the side of the road in Honduras—but that one got me in trouble! I was in Honduras with Compassion International for a mission trip. On our last day, we had taken a few hours to go shopping at the market. Unfortunately, I wasn't feeling very well, so I just laid down on the side of the road as I was waiting for the rest of our crew to finish shopping. I ended up dozing off. When I awoke, a military officer was standing a few yards away with a machine gun in his hands, looking at me. One of the Compassion reps quickly came over to get me and said I needed to get up because I couldn't sleep there.

My experiences with sleeping on the street have always helped me empathize with homeless men and women. I can understand being startled by noises. I know what it means to wake up cold. I have felt the rejection of people when they tell you that you can't sleep in certain places. Sleeping on the street has definitely changed me and my perception of the homeless.

The Canyon

On the third day of my spiritual journey, I ended up at the Grand Canyon. I arrived at Grand Canyon National Park at around ten p.m. I parked my car and started walking toward the outer rim of the canyon. I walked very cautiously toward the rim because it was very dark. I couldn't see more than a few feet in front of me. Eventually, I made it to the edge of the canyon and sat down, allowing my feet to hang out over the rim and dangle into space. It was a great feeling. I sat there for several hours, praying and asking God to use me to save people.

At one point I looked up and found everything had changed. My eyes had adjusted to the dark and I was able to start seeing things. I could now see the outline of the north rim. I could make out the shapes of rocks. But what really got me was the depth of the blackness in the bottom of the canyon and the haze that seemed to hover over it. I must admit what I saw brought fear into my life. I was actually scared, not because it was dark, but because I was feeling the Lord convicting me to go into the valley and fight evil, spiritual forces for the souls of lost people.

What happened that night to my eyes can happen with your eyes, but only if you give yourself enough time. Many people want to reach out to the lost, but all they see is darkness. They don't see shapes, outlines, or people. They only see the blackness. This blackness brings about fear in people and, rather than attack it, they flee from it.

I encourage you to look into the darkness, pray, and give your spiritual eyes time to adjust. The blackness isn't worth fearing, but what you see when your eyes adjust does merit fear—a fear that needs to be conquered. When I first sat down at the Grand Canyon, I couldn't see anything. But the longer I sat there and the more I prayed, the more my eyes were able to pick out things. There are a lot of people wandering in the darkness. Don't be afraid of what you initially can't see. Give your eyes time to adjust, and then go into the valley to battle.

After a few hours I decided to crawl into my van and get some sleep. At five a.m. my alarm went off, so I got up and headed for the rim again. At this point it was still dark, but I knew the sun would start to rise soon and I would witness the majesty of God. And that I did. Here are the very words from my journal that morning:

> The sun is rising over the Grand Canyon as I write. It is inspiring to see the beauty of the canyon unfold before my eyes. God, you are shooting light beams into the darkest crevices in the canyon and bringing them to life. You are taking this lifeless, gray, foggy canyon and radiating your light through it. You have now totally covered this canyon with your light just as you totally cover the valley of sin with your grace.

The night before, all I could see was darkness and a valley of sin. But that morning I received a conviction from the Lord that his grace can cover it all. With that in mind, what are we waiting for? There is no sin God can't forgive. There is no sinner he can't pardon. There is no prisoner he can't set free. There is nothing so black that his light can't penetrate. Therefore, we need to rush into the valley of darkness and allow the Son to come up.

My Journey

After the sun came up over the canyon, I went on a hike. I hiked down Angel Trail toward the bottom of the Grand Canyon. After a couple of miles, I sat down and prayed some more. I laid it all before the Lord—my thoughts, fears, anger, sin, regrets, family, career, heart, tears, and will. God and I went a couple of rounds in the ring until I was finally willing to give up and give in. At that point, it was as if I felt a huge burden release from my shoulders and my heart. God took his gloves off and used his hands to lift things off of my back.

Then it was as if he gave me a huge hug and said, "Go! Go for me and remember I am always with you." At that point, I felt a newfound freedom and passion. I wanted to immediately conquer the world. From there I went off the beaten path and tried to climb up the side of the Grand Canyon. It was an adventure that was breathtaking. I climbed straight up through a crevice for what seemed like forever. At one point I stopped and looked down and about wet myself. I was so high up that it felt like I was hovering above the canyon. It was scary to look down, but it was also one of the biggest rushes I had ever felt. It was exhilarating. I eventually climbed back down and got back onto Angel Trail.

I left the Grand Canyon and ventured to Hoover Dam. From there I spent a day in Las Vegas, and then I drove up I-15 through Utah and caught I-70 toward Denver. I have driven to all four corners of the continental United States. I have seen a ton of beautiful things along those roads, but I have to admit the best stretch of road I have ever traveled is I-70 from Utah to Denver. There are so many different landscapes: picturesque plateaus, colorful canyons, white water rivers, and snow-capped Rockies.

My spiritual journey was a week that changed my life. I discovered what it meant to be on a journey. Let me encourage you as I conclude this chapter and this book. You are on a journey. A journey that never ends. It starts with your birth, changes with your death, and continues through eternity. Don't get so caught up in life that you miss this journey or so caught up in your own journey that you fail to help other people with theirs.

Most Christians only think of their final destination. They are so consumed with getting to heaven that they forget to live. They often act like the little kid in the car who constantly asks, "Are we there yet?" If that is what you are asking, then you are going to miss so much of what God has in store for you. My spiritual journey taught me a very valuable lesson in life. Most people miss the journey because they are looking for the destination. My destination is simply the celebrating point of my journey.

Enjoy the journey!

QUESTIONS TO PONDER

Do you do things on the fly or do you have to plan? What was the last thing you did at the spur of the moment? How did it make you feel?

Where do you go to find peace and quiet? Do you take God there with you?

How has your opinion of homeless people changed while reading this book?

Are you afraid of the dark? How has your opinion of lost people changed while reading this book? What are you doing now to reach out to those in the valley?

Are you inclined to ask, "Are we there yet?" Or do you take the scenic route in life? Set aside a couple of hours or even a whole day and take a mini spiritual journey of your own. Go to a lake, a park, or even a city. Go someplace with just God, your Word, and a journal. Spend some time with God and then get back into the valley—because there are people there who need you.

Scriptures to Study

    Matthew 14:25–33
    1 Kings 19:1–18
    Luke 9:1–6

Thoughts and Prayers

Spend some time reflecting not just on this chapter, but also on this entire book. What has changed in your life while you have been reading it? Are you finding yourself having more opportunities to share your faith? Do you find that your heart is hurting more for people and your eyes are noticing more spiritual things? Finish up by setting some goals for yourself, your walk with God, and your evangelistic impact on the world. (I would love to hear your thoughts, reflections, and stories. If God has been working on you or if you have some stories of people you have encountered, please share them with me by posting them at www.staroutreach.net)

Journal

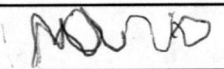

Conclusion
Where Are They Now?

Did I Do Any Good?

I often get asked if I feel like I accomplish anything through my encounters. People question if there was any value to my evangelism because I can't say every encounter led a person to Christ. So was my work in vain? I don't think so. Luke 8 talks about a farmer who went out to sow some seed. The farmer threw the seed all over the place. He threw some on the path, some on rocky soil, some on the weeds, and some on the good soil.

There is an often-overlooked part of this parable. Many people focus on the type of soil, but I want to focus on the farmer. His number one concern wasn't about looking for the best soil. His concern was about planting seeds. I throw seeds wherever I can and let God do the growing. I would rather throw a seed and have it not take root than never give the seed a chance.

Where Are They Now?

Honestly, I can't tell you where most of the people I've encountered are because many of them were just people on the street. But I do want to give you a rundown of all the people I've mentioned in this book, for informational and prayer reasons.

Ybor City: Homeless boy, two teenagers, and a stripper. Unfortunately, that is the only thing I can tell you about them. My prayer is the homeless boy went home, the two boys found what they really needed, and the stripper kicked her drug habit and is taking care of her daughter.

Kristie: I hate the fact that the last memory I have of Kristie is her turning away from the message of the gospel. Pray wherever she is in the world that she will hear the message of Christ again.

Bea: Pray Bea realizes that, yes, she is a sinner, but is loved by God and can find forgiveness.

Melissa: Pray she has found her way back home and is sharing ice-cream with her parents.

Lucas: Pray Lucas has picked up the Jesus crutch.

Rickster: Rick returned to his faith that night at the conference. About a year later I was in Palm Springs again and I ran into Rick at McDonald's. We shared in a great conversation and he told me he was doing really well.

Conclusion: Where Are They Now?

Yellow Dress: I think about the girl in the yellow dress often. Please pray for her and the children of Haiti. It is a place of devastation. Pray for the children to find food, clothing, shelter, and safety. And especially pray they find Jesus.

Alice and Travis: I still see them all the time because I have a picture of them I keep in my office that reminds me to pray for them. Pray for them to find shelter, freedom from their addictions, and healing for Alice's skin disease and that they continue to see the love God has for them.

John and his three friends: Pray for the loneliness and pain we saw in these men. Pray for John and his relationship with his daughter. Pray for Christians who will stop and give them Christ.

Tracy #1: I still see her eyes through the picture in my office. I see a young girl who is searching. Pray she finds a church that will love and accept her.

Tracy #2: Tracey is doing well. I see her at church every weekend. She loves the Lord, but still struggles because of her past addictions. She is tempted often and falls occasionally. Pray for her to have strength.

Tate: Tate is now a very healthy young man. He is now almost five and runs, plays, jumps, laughs, and asks for McDonald's like a good old American boy. His favorite thing is to wrestle with his older brother and me.

Abbey: She is doing extremely well. She is a beautiful young lady with long braided hair. She loves coloring and playing with her sister.

Kris: I haven't seen Kris since high school. Last I heard she is doing really well. Let me take a moment here to make sure I say Kris wasn't a bad girl. She was actually a very good Christian young woman. She just made a bad judgment call. For the most part, Kris is a person after whom to model your faith.

Ally: Ally ended up moving away to Pennsylvania. She got closer to the Lord but, unfortunately, to my knowledge didn't make it all the way. An interesting thing, though, is while ministering to her I met her friend, and my bartender, Shannon. Shannon, while working the bar, would join in conversations with us. With Shannon it stuck, and I witnessed her give her life to the Lord. The joy on her face was amazing when she came up out of her baptism.

Joab and Judy: I continue to pray for Joab and Judy. I pray for them to meet a Christian couple who will accept them and befriend them. Pray for the same thing. Pray when they hit rock bottom they will have a Christian friend to whom to turn.

Stacey: Pray for Stacey. I went back to the bar to try to find her, but she had quit. I haven't seen her since our meeting in my office. Pray her daughter is doing well, and pray they fill the hole in their hearts with Jesus.

Ashley: I ran into the youth pastor who put on the festival about a year later, and he informed me Ashley had gotten plugged in to his group. He said she was very involved and growing in the Lord.

James: My church and I failed James. I thought he had gotten plugged in, but I realized I was sorely mistaken when I got a letter from him. We had sent out a letter to everyone who had attended our church just letting him or her know what was going on at church.

Conclusion: Where Are They Now?

He got the letter and sent a reply back to me that said, "Josh, I'm glad to hear your church is growing, but I'm still dying. I still drink every day, cut every day, and live in depression. I'm glad you are growing, but I'm dying." When I got that letter, it killed me. Since then I have stayed in written contact with James, doing my best to encourage him to find life in Christ.

Tyler: I haven't seen Tyler since that concert, but it was so good to hear he is doing great and going into the ministry. Pray for his new ministry.

Family: My family is doing awesome. I can't believe how far they have all come spiritually. My mom and dad go to Bible study every week. My brother and his family are all very involved at their church. He and his wife are youth sponsors at their church and have been on several mission trips. Last Christmas I was blown away because we sat around and talked about church and God all day. It was amazing.

Amy: I've never seen Amy again, but I've encountered many more people just like her, and unfortunately I've missed too many other opportunities. Pray for Amy that someone else talked to her about God and pray you will not miss the Amys God puts in your path.

Again, I can't tell you where they all are, but I do know in most cases I threw some seed out for God to water. Join with me and throw some seeds…let's get dirty!

Pleasant Word

To order additional copies of this title call:
1-877-421-READ (7323)
or please visit our web site at
www.pleasantwordbooks.com

If you enjoyed this quality custom published book,
drop by our web site for more books and information.

www.winepressgroup.com
"Your partner in custom publishing."